CONQUER
THE CHAOS

c.3

CONQUER THE CHAOS

HOW TO GROW A SUCCESSFUL SMALL BUSINESS

without Going Crazy

Clate Mask
Scott Martineau

WILEY

John Wiley & Sons, Inc.

For general information on our other products and services or for technical support, please contact our Customer Care Department within the United States at (800) 762-2974, outside the United States at (317) 572-3993 or fax (317) 572-4002.

Wiley also publishes its books in a variety of electronic formats. Some content that appears in print may not be available in electronic books. For more information about Wiley products, visit our web site at www.wiley.com.

ISBN 978-0-470-59932-7 (cloth)
ISBN 978-0-470-64229-0 (ebk)
ISBN 978-0-470-64230-6 (ebk)
ISBN 978-0-470-64231-3 (ebk)

Printed in the United States of America.

10 9 8 7 6 5 4 3 2

To Charisse and Andee for all your support,
love, and understanding.

CONTENTS

FOREWORD

Catastrophe is not too light a word to describe what happens when somebody decides in a moment of unreflective zeal to start a business.

In this book, Clate Mask and Scott Martineau tell the story about as eloquently as I've ever heard it told.

Not only that, but these wonderful friends of mine, both passionate entrepreneurs, describe their story in such an authentic way that you, the reader, can't help but be moved to do for yourself what Scott and Clate have learned to do for themselves, their thousands of clients, and the jubilant, passionate, committed people who work for them at their great and growing company, Infusionsoft, to overcome the confusion, to redefine their game, to pursue what most would see as impossible, and to succeed today in the worst of times, as though the economic reality that has taken its toll on countless thousands of small businesses and large is just another obstacle to get around.

And get around it Scott and Clate have done indeed.

As their determination to grow, to become the small business growth leader worldwide, continues unabated, these two restless young guys certainly have set a template for the rest of us to emulate.

The tragedy of most small business failures, Clate and Scott tell us, is that those failures didn't have to happen.

There are answers to chaos. There are methods behind the seeming madness. There are systems that need to be deployed—for lead generation and lead conversion and people development and much, much more. And when these systems are invented and then deployed, new lessons are learned—lessons that Scott and Clate speak about unabashedly within this book; they speak so enthusiastically, like a couple of kids discovering a new game or a new toy, that you'll wonder why you had never thought of them before.

And that's one of the reasons I love this book. It's not simply another business story like the many we've been told. It's a passionate prescription from a couple of entrepreneurial ideologues, two guys who spend every waking hour creating, and when that doesn't work, breaking it down and creating some more.

What's more, for you reading this along with me, the lessons and prescriptions that Scott and Clate are passing along to you here come to the page through hard service. In their own words, they tell us of the mistakes they've made: the truly big ones— not just the little things that entrepreneurs bump into in the dead of night, but the big, monstrous ones that can take you down faster than a speeding bullet, and take your breath away.

Yes, this book is real.

And that's why it's so damn good.

Because, even as you're reading it, the story is going on, every day in Arizona where Infusionsoft gets up every morning to take its daily tally. How did we do yesterday? the gang at Infusionsoft asks. How can we do it better today? they all inquire. That is another reason why this book will astonish you.

It's a living story. It's not over by a long shot. It's working its wonderful way forward even as we speak, and leaving us with the unanswerable question: Will Scott and Clate make it? Will this story end with a bang or a whimper? This isn't a book about IBM. This is a book about a young start-up, on its way to greatness or disaster. And, I swear, you'll find yourself—as I did reading this book—putting your money on its authors.

Scott and Clate are onto something—something big. It's called entrepreneurship in the raw, and it's what created our country, and is creating our country even now as we speak.

—Michael E. Gerber
Founder, Michael E. Gerber Companies,
Origination, The Dreaming Room;
Author of the E-Myth books and *The Most Successful Small Business in the World*

PREFACE

Seven years ago we found ourselves surrounded by chaos, worried whether we would ever get our new business off the ground. Sure, we had dreams of finding our entrepreneurial freedom, but at the time we were just trying to keep the lights on.

It was August 2002. Our custom software company received an interesting phone call. It was Friday at 5:00 P.M. and the four of us were getting ready to wrap up the week. We'd ordered pizza, and it had just arrived when the phone rang. Well, the last thing we wanted to do was talk to anyone. But we needed sales, so Clate decided to pick up the phone.

No sooner had he rattled off his greeting than the man on the other end shouted, "I have *pain*! Can you help me?" Then the man paused.

Clate's mind was reeling with concerns. Was this a prank? Did this guy even know what number he had dialed? Was this a customer? What was Clate supposed to do about someone's pain? Shouldn't he call a doctor?

Eventually, Clate got to the root of this man's problem. The caller, Reed Hoisington, was searching for a software program that would more effectively manage his contacts. He was trying to follow up with his prospects and customers, but he was making a lot of mistakes.

On this particular day, Reed had mistakenly sent a special, reduced-price offer to a group of people, including many folks who had already bought that product at full price. Customers were angry, demanding refunds and Reed was in *pain*!

The irony is, at the time of Reed's phone call, we too had pain! We were struggling to acquire new customers and our struggles were seriously impacting our home lives to the extent that we faced the very real possibility of going out of business.

But, despite the challenges we were personally experiencing, we were learning some very important lessons; lessons so powerful, that following their teachings will free any small business owner from the chaos we nearly all find ourselves immersed in. This is the very purpose of this book.

Now, at this point, you might be thinking, "Well, how do you know I'm experiencing chaos? What makes you think I'm not completely satisfied with the way things are going in my business?"

If that's the case—if you are contentedly growing your business *and* you enjoy your lifestyle, then great! You can stop reading right now. If you feel you are getting all the benefits from your business that you could possibly hope for, this book is not for you.

This book is for the entrepreneur who went into business looking for freedom but found chaos rather than finding

- More *Time* to spend with their families
- More *Money*
- More *Control* to live life the way they want, and
- The satisfaction of achieving their *Purpose*

This book is for entrepreneurs who feel trapped, controlled, and consumed by their business.

If you're emphatically or even reluctantly agreeing that yes, this describes your situation, then we've got news for you: you're not alone. The vast majority of small business owners are struggling just to keep their heads above water. In fact, most of us tend to clump together in a boat of survival, hanging on for dear life, putting on a happy face as we get more and more bogged down by our businesses.

Let us show you what we mean. A couple of years ago, we headed out on the road speaking to large groups of entrepreneurs in Los Angeles, Chicago, New York, and Orlando.

At each stop, we asked the audience the same question: "How many of you are satisfied with your small business?"

Of 1,574 small business owners, three raised their hands. Three. *Three*! Some of these individuals had been in business for more than 20 years!

What was going on? And why were so many people in business for themselves if they weren't getting satisfaction out of it?

After some reflection, we realized we already knew the answer to the question. Because, in addition to working with tens of thousands of small business owners, we too have felt the fears, pains, worry and stress of small business ownership. We've been in the trenches. And together we've experienced things that only other entrepreneurs will ever understand.

The results of the "Are you satisfied?" poll stuck with us. So we made it a habit to ask the question whenever we could. The more we asked the question, the more we heard of business owners' dissatisfaction, and the more we knew we *had* to write this book to help small business owners all over the world.

WHY ARE WE TELLING THIS STORY?

We love entrepreneurs. We love their tenacity, ambition, work ethic, innovation and creativity. We love that they have the guts to cast aside fear and criticism in order to go out and do something bold and daring that will create a ton of value, bring satisfaction to their souls and produce opportunity for themselves and all those they employ.

We love entrepreneurs! And we *hate* seeing them fail. We hate seeing their doors close. We hate seeing them lose their hope. We hate seeing their confidence squashed, their financial lives ruined and their relationships shattered. And we hate seeing their creative fire doused by the torrential waters of harsh reality.

We hate it—because we have been there ourselves and feel a tight bond with the entrepreneurs fighting to get through each day and find their freedom.

You see, almost immediately after graduating from college, we found ourselves in the middle of our own chaos. Real chaos. The kind that is gripping small business owners all over the world. As we joined forces in a startup computer software company, we started to truly live the pains and struggles entrepreneurs regularly cope with. Before long, we were beaten down and grasping for answers.

Fortunately, we had a great advantage. In 2003, our company switched from being a custom software business to providing one standard product to entrepreneurs. We developed a software program to automate sales, marketing, customer management and billing processes for small business owners. Our advantage was that we had the good fortune of working with great entrepreneurs—hundreds of them, actually—in the process of creating this software program. Our software was saving them time and helping them make more money without needing to add extra expenses or hire new employees. Their experience, input, and help were invaluable to our product development. And we learned a ton about small business success as we worked with these entrepreneurs.

Then, a phenomenal thing happened—we started using our own software in our business! Once we did that, the light bulb turned on. We had something great. And more than that, we had unwittingly discovered several of the strategies for conquering the chaos and achieving the dreams we'd nearly given up.

After that, we were in a prime position for learning how to fight *and* conquer the chaos of business ownership. We worked with more and more entrepreneurs and we learned the reasons why the chaos exists and how to defeat it.

A BETTER WAY OF LIFE FOR SMALL BUSINESS OWNERS

In addition to our experiences, years of interacting with small business owners brought us to some simple but significant conclusions. We watched the same mistakes being made over and over again. We saw seemingly popular companies close their doors for the last time. And, we observed other companies skyrocket for no apparent reason.

What we learned is that the strategies for conquering the chaos and growing a successful business are not unique to one industry, company or business owner. Success is determined by the use of predictable, repeatable, simple actions. But not just any actions—the right actions.

Ultimately, these strategies developed into the focal point for our company. They became the driving force, the culmination of everything we had dreamed of doing for entrepreneurs. For years we've developed and refined these strategies so they would provide the most and best value for the entrepreneur.

HOW THIS BOOK WILL LEAD YOU TO FREEDOM

This book does not contain stuffy, official research. Each of the six strategies, and all of the examples and stories are part

of an ongoing case study. We live the proof of the six strategies every day. And we have watched in amazement as one
company after another learns these basic truths, applies them
and enjoys success.

The first three chapters of this book include the *real* story
of small business ownership. They include the Quest for Freedom, the fear, the pain, the overwhelming feelings, and the
emotional struggle. It's the forced humility of the small business owner. It's the story of the neglected family, mounting
debts and bitter partnerships. But it's also the story of how
chaos happens and how to combat it.

In Chapter 1, you'll learn why millions of individuals choose
to become entrepreneurs, even though they might know the
struggles they'll soon experience. This chapter also includes
the hope and ambition new entrepreneurs feel and seasoned
entrepreneurs wish they could remember.

Chapter 2 is an explanation on the origins of chaos. We show
you why chaos is inevitable—no matter how skillful an entrepreneur might be.

As you read Chapter 3, you'll realize that running from chaos
is futile. Chaos *must* be met head-on if you ever hope to find
your freedom. This chapter helps you evaluate your relationship with chaos and prepares you to gain control of your
business.

In Section 2, the Mindset strategies for conquering chaos are
introduced. Because chaos is as much a state of mind as a state
of affairs, Chapters 4, 5, and 6 teach you how to overcome fear,
anxiety, frustration, and skepticism in order to make the necessary changes in your business.

Hand-in-hand with the Mindset strategies, Section 3
presents the Systems strategies. In this section, you will learn
why business systems are critical to liberating you from the
demands of your business. After reading Chapters 7 through
9, you will understand the concepts of centralizing, following
up, and automating as important keys to the growth of your
business.

In the final section, Chapters 10 and 11 demonstrate how to avoid the backslide into chaos and how the six strategies lead you to your freedom. These chapters illustrate the entrepreneurial dream, and how you can easily achieve that dream if you're willing to implement the lessons we, and other small business owners have learned.

With the strategies included in this book, you will find the power to turn around your business and your life. You will discover there is a better, more productive way to run your business. And you will learn that by implementing these six strategies, you can conquer the chaos, find the time, money, control and purpose to live life on your terms, and truly enjoy being an entrepreneur again.

Acknowledgments

We would like to express appreciation to the many people who have contributed to the realization of our dream: to revolutionize the way small businesses grow.

To early mentors Reed Hoisington, Joe Polish, and Perry Marshall for their marketing savvy, entrepreneurship, acumen and continued support. You guys know what it means to be an entrepreneur and your advice helped us become comfortable in the trenches of entrepreneurship.

To subsequent mentors Michael Gerber, Bill Glazer, Dan Kennedy and Dan Sullivan, for teaching us what it takes to go from entrepreneurs to successful business owners. Your skills in business management, marketing strategy, and life-balance were essential for us to build a multi-million dollar business.

To software mentors Pat Sullivan and Geoffrey Moore for your product marketing and positioning genius that continue to help us achieve our vision for Infusionsoft to become the "Quickbooks of sales and marketing software."

We want to thank our employees for making the dream, vision, purpose and mission of Infusionsoft a reality.

To entrepreneurs everywhere, for having the guts to do hard stuff, create value, and live the thrill of life as a business owner.

To our parents, both sets, for your love, encouragement, and support of our dreams.

Lastly, to our own families for your support, especially in those times when our Mindset strategies were out of whack and our Systems strategies were lacking.

CONQUER THE CHAOS

Section I

THE QUEST FOR FREEDOM

1
THE ENTREPRENEURIAL REVOLUTION

The difference between the great and good societies and the regressing, deteriorating societies is largely in terms of the entrepreneurial opportunity and the number of such people in the society. I think everyone would agree that the most valuable 100 people to bring into a deteriorating society would be not 100 chemists, or politicians, or professors, or engineers, but rather 100 entrepreneurs.

—Abraham Maslow

B y the time you finish reading this chapter, 140 people will have started their own business. If you read the entire book straight through, another 1,000 business owners will have joined the ranks of entrepreneurship, and that's in the United States alone.[1]

Entrepreneurship is exploding all around us. Once considered a profession for a few rare, perhaps eccentric souls, entrepreneurship is today a widely respected profession.

Certainly, as an entrepreneur, you've noticed the growing interest in small business ownership. You have friends who are entrepreneurs. Perhaps a brother, aunt, or cousin has started a business. Your neighbor down the street owns her own business. If you have children, they may be gearing up to follow in your footsteps.

Whether you realize it or not, we are in the middle of a revolution—the Entrepreneurial Revolution. This revolution is not intended to overthrow the government or establish a new nation. This revolution is about how we work and how business is done. As an entrepreneur, you are part of this revolution. Unfortunately, the outcome of your involvement in this revolution is yet to be decided.

---

[1] According to the U.S. Census Bureau, there are nearly 30 million small businesses in the United States alone, and approximately 600,000 additional businesses are added every year.

Like all revolutions, the Entrepreneurial Revolution will have massive casualties. This book is meant to help you successfully participate in the Entrepreneurial Revolution, without becoming a casualty.

THE PATH TO REVOLUTION

Revolutions don't just start of their own accord. Nobody wakes up one morning and thinks, "I'd sure like to be part a revolution." The American Revolution didn't gain instant popularity because someone thought the United States should be independent. Quite the contrary. Less than half the country was committed to the cause. The other half was clinging desperately to the safety and security of familiarity.

The French Revolution was not an attempt to follow suit. People were starving. Disease and death were sweeping through the masses. Without a revolution, thousands more would have perished. But once again, there were many hesitant to embrace such change.

For any revolution to occur, three factors must be present (see Figure 1.1). Within the last few years, the same factors present during the bloodiest of revolutions made their way into the American economy, creating a fertile ground for the Entrepreneurial Revolution.

ANY REVOLUTION	AMERICAN REVOLUTION	ENTREPRENEURIAL REVOLUTION
• Loss of Security	• No Representation	• Corporate Distrust
• Power Shift	• Continental Congress	• The Internet
• Promise of Something Better	• The Declaration of Independence	• The Overnight Success Story

Figure 1.1 The Three Elements of a Revolution

6

So what are these factors? They are:

1. Oppression from Authority
2. A Shift in Power, and
3. The Promise of Something Better

If you know your history, then you know the American Revolution was triggered by over-taxation, misrepresentation, and unjust domination from British colony leaders. The French Revolution was a result of the rich getting richer, the poor getting poorer, the lost voice of the commoner, and the fear of imminent death. Similarly, the Entrepreneurial Revolution would never have gained momentum if the country hadn't been primed for change.

THE OPPRESSION: CORPORATE DISTRUST

In the generation past, many folks spent their entire careers at a single company, retiring after 40 years of dedicated service to someone else. To these folks, long-term employment with the company was the safe, wise, stable thing to do.

Over time, large businesses and corporations dominated American culture and held all the power in our economy. This corporate dominance led to the mistaken belief that job security meant working for a well-established company instead of being great at what you do. If you wanted to get ahead in life, you worked 9 to 5 in a predictable, stable environment. Now to entrepreneurs, that notion is revolting.

When disputes with employees or customers arose, the corporation nearly always won. Realizing there wasn't much they could do about it, the population dealt with corporate injustices by simply accepting them. Even the most outraged of victims had to think carefully before rocking the boat. Perhaps influenced by the effects of the Great Depression and several other economic backslides, older generations believed that if you had a "good" job, you'd better keep it.

Now, however, the days of loyal employment are over. Working 40 years for the same company is practically unheard of. Corporate horror stories dominate the headlines. Stories of corporate scandals, shareholder fraud, greedy chief executive officers (CEOs) and failed 401(k) retirement plans have victimized employees and the general public, creating distrust and cynicism toward corporations.

It seems everybody has friends who were "let go just before retirement so the corporation could save some of its pension costs." Corporate employees watch in alarm as their jobs get shipped overseas. They feel the pressure of the global market, which is requiring them to do more and work harder in their corporate positions. Large corporate layoffs have mercilessly dispelled the belief that a good job is worth keeping, no matter what the cost.

The bottom line is that corporate employees are working harder and feeling less of the benefits. If nothing else, they're certainly questioning the long-term benefits. Heck, they've even lost the belief that all their dollars paid into Social Security will ever come back to them.

And so, the institutions (corporate and governmental) that our parents believed would provide security have broken down. Unique corporate cultures were replaced with office politics and vicious backstabbing. Workers for Corporate America feel jilted, a little burned, and taken for a ride to a certain extent. Rather than relying on their corporation to care for their needs as employees and in retirement, many Americans face a reality of corporate disillusionment.

The more disillusionment increases, the more primed folks are to join the Entrepreneurial Revolution. All told, this loss of security is dramatically changing the landscape of the American workforce. College graduates are learning that the corporation isn't going to create their stability. They've learned that entrepreneurs create their own stability. So they start businesses from their dorm rooms, hoping the business will catch fire and prevent them from ever having to take a job.

Corporate disillusionment has altered everything our parents taught us about working in "stable" jobs at big companies. As a result, people are motivated to take action. So they turn in the one direction they feel they have the most control: inward.

THE POWER SHIFT: THE INTERNET AGE

No matter how determined an individual might be, real change—revolutionary change—is not possible until strengthened by the masses. Sure, it only takes one voice to put things in motion. But power comes from a multitude working together.

During the American Revolution, it was the strength of the entire Congress that led men to battle. For the Entrepreneurial Revolution, the rally cry came through the most unique medium to date: the Internet.

If you had to sum up the one big thing that is driving this revolution, it is the Internet. Pure and simple. The widespread adoption of the Internet over the past decade has changed everything. The Internet:

- Gives a loud voice to the common person
- Allows a small business to look big
- Makes information readily accessible
- Opens a global marketplace to Joe and Jill in Podunk, Montana
- Breaks down the barriers to entry by eliminating the need for piles of capital
- Connects businesses and their customers through speedy communication
- Unchains entrepreneurs from their desks so they can work from anywhere
- Makes it possible for anyone to leverage and profit from their expertise
- Simplifies the complicated, costly "distribution channels" of old

- Empowers entrepreneurs to transact online, in their sleep and out of the country
- Puts the power of automation in the hands of the little guy
- Enables efficiencies for small businesses that used to exist only in big businesses

As product review sites made their debut, the power of corporate control was shifted into the hands of the average Joe. No longer were consumers subjected to the official reviews and opinions of industry experts. Now, consumers gleaned all the information they needed from individuals just like them.

For the entrepreneur, this shift in power made small business ownership easier to achieve and less expensive to start. We won't address all the benefits individually, but rather skim over a few of the most significant.

INFORMATION IS READILY ACCESSIBLE

Aspiring entrepreneurs can now quickly research a new business idea. They can test the demand for their products using a few hundred bucks and a good Google AdWords campaign. They can do quick surveys by email, study potential competitors' websites and even "mystery shop" the competition to find out where the gaps in the market exist that they can turn around and fill—for a profit.

This kind of information is available to everyone. You don't need nearly the time or capital that were once required to prove the viability of your idea. Gone are the long days, weeks, and months in the library, driving around from store to store, demon-dialing the competition to see what the customer experience is like. You can amass all of that information quickly and inexpensively, from the privacy of your own home.

SMALL BUSINESSES LOOK BIG

Now that small businesses have been empowered with information, they can compete with the big guys. A website, advanced software, and a strong, focused market offering will enable a small company to beat the pants off a bigger company. No heavy capital investment is needed. No store front is required. All the business owner needs is technology, passion and a good product or service to spread the word and she's in business.

When businesses required a brick and mortar shop, customers knew exactly how big a business was and could guess the success of the company by the size, location, and number of staff. Now, entrepreneurs are running entire companies out of their basements, and online consumers are none the wiser.

As long as there's a demand for their products and services, small business owners can achieve incredible success, no matter what large company might open its doors two blocks down the street.

THE MARKETPLACE IS GLOBAL

In 1998, Clate was in his MBA program. At the time, his older sister had started a business that made and sold a special kind of baby bow that allowed moms to swap out swatches of color-coordinated fabric in a lycra headband. One bow, three headbands, about 8 bucks. Her friends were buying them fast and things were really catching on.

But Clate's sister needed to get her bows into the retail distribution channel. She asked Clate to help her out, so he made calls to buyers at Nordstrom, Dillard's, and a few other department stores. The problem was the classic chicken-and-egg dilemma that so many entrepreneurs with products face. The buyer won't put them on their shelves unless enough units have sold to demonstrate the demand. His sister had sold hundreds, maybe thousands of bows, but that was a drop in the bucket to retail buyers.

So, Clate's sister was stuck. She could either invest tens or hundreds of thousands of dollars to get her product developed in mass quantities and distributed through specialty shops (which would build up unit sales to demonstrate demand to the big buyers) or she could fold up shop and lose the couple of years of blood, sweat, tears (and money!) she and her partner had invested.

As Clate's sister wrestled with this problem, Clate was in an MBA marketing class where they talked about distribution. After class, he went up to his professor, explained his sister's problem, and asked what she should do. The answer was profound.

"I feel for your sister, Clate. But if you guys can solve that problem, you will be billionaires."

Just a couple of years earlier, the problem *had* been solved, but Clate didn't realize it. A guy named Pierre Omidyar had created an online auction website. After the first item (a broken laser pen) was sold, eBay was officially in business. Since then, consumers have auctioned everything from brussels sprouts to airplanes to countries.

Without the Internet, global markets would be inaccessible to any but the biggest businesses. Proximity would be a key factor in determining which businesses consumers would buy from. One-man shops would be overrun by the cheaper prices (and often inferior quality) of big businesses. In other words, small business owners would be stuck with "distribution" problems as they tried to build their businesses.

So, we love the power of the Internet. We love the value and opportunity it provides entrepreneurs. And we love the Entrepreneurial Revolution that is happening all around us because of it. But before we get carried away praising the Internet, we'd like to issue one word of warning. As much as we love the Internet, it is also a huge contributor to entrepreneurial chaos, which you will discover in the next chapter. For now, we'll move on to the last revolutionary factor.

THE PROMISE: THE OVERNIGHT SUCCESS STORY

The Fourth of July, celebrated as Independence Day, is not the day the United States won its freedom. The American Revolution had only just begun when this historically significant day rolled around. In actuality, the Fourth of July is the day attributed to the signing of the Declaration of Independence, long before independence was actually won.

Imagine that. More remembered than the day the colonists won their freedom is the day they declared their independence. Now, historians may correct us all they want to, but we believe this act to be significant because it gave the colonists something tangible to hold on to. It gave them a cause. It gave them hope. After all the frustration, fear, and pain, finally they held the promise of something better.

For the Entrepreneurial Revolution, the concept is the same. If corporate disillusionment provided the fuel and the Internet provided the means to start a revolution, then all that was left was to light the match. And the match—the spark that ignites the bonfire, the promise of something better—is a little thing called *The Perceived Overnight Success Story*.

The media certainly seems to be propagating the Entrepreneurial Revolution by sharing story after story of entrepreneurs who go from the garage to the penthouse almost instantaneously. There's nothing they like better than to share the unlikely tale of an "average" person who rises quickly to fame or fortune.

Now, right or wrong, workers in Corporate America look at the stories of successful entrepreneurs and they see "an overnight success." They see all the benefits that come to a successful entrepreneur: time, money, control, and purpose. But they don't see the chaos, the monumental struggle to build a successful business.

Instead, they see the work schedule flexibility they crave, and they bitterly resent their boss for not allowing it. They see the successful entrepreneur buy a new car or new home, and they feel a twinge of jealousy. They see the blossomed creativity of the entrepreneur who advances their ideas in the marketplace—and they harbor feelings of resentment when their own ideas are not appreciated at work. They see entrepreneurs accomplishing their dreams—and they kick themselves for not taking action when they "thought of that idea first."

These are all subtle, internal forces that decidedly tip the scale in favor of entrepreneurship. Granted, most corporate workers don't pay attention to the years of blood, sweat, and tears that preceded the entrepreneur's "overnight success." But in a game of perception, that gross oversight doesn't matter. Corporate workers feel their work life is just plain unfair, and they, too, reach out for the promise of a better, more satisfying life. A promise that sounds like this:

"I've always wanted to start a business; it's time for me to pursue my dream."

"Joe went for it and look at him now. If he can do it, I certainly can."

"With all the layoffs around here, now's as good a time as any."

"I want the flexibility to call my own shots, work when I want and spend time with the family."

"Honey, I just can't take it anymore. I *have* to start my own thing."

"I'll start it on the side and build it up until we can afford for me to quit my job."

"Let's find a way to line up health insurance, get a little more in savings, and take the plunge."

These are the conversations going on around kitchen tables across America. You probably said something like this yourself before starting your business. And if you haven't ventured out on your own yet, you still *feel* the reality of these statements, don't you?

THE HIERARCHY OF FREEDOMS

So the stage has been set. The three factors all perfectly combined to create revolutionary conditions; and the population responded by turning to small business ownership in droves.

But the cold, hard truth is that this is *still* a revolution. With any revolution, you have to expect casualties. Even if a revolution brings about positive change, it cannot be done without someone getting hurt. In this case, it's the entrepreneurs themselves who end up "wounded."

Payroll pressure, customer fires, employee hassles, challenges at home, inner struggles about whether you can pull it off, finding new customers, collecting on invoices, paying the bills, juggling technology, and, in effect, running 90 miles an hour with your hair on fire—that is the reality of small business ownership for the vast majority of entrepreneurs.

Even as new entrepreneurs emerge, others are closing their doors. As an excited college student looks forward to her new endeavor as business owner, others are wondering what they got themselves into. But new or old, experienced or just beginning, entrepreneurs will continue to press forward. Why?

Because finally, they have *a chance to find their own freedom;* and that's certainly a goal worth fighting for. That quest for freedom is the reason we jump into entrepreneurship.

A couple years ago, Clate was talking to his son, Tanner, who was 10 years old at the time. They were talking about business and what Tanner might want to do when he grows up. As Clate asked him the question, Tanner quickly blurted out, "I want to do what Jake's dad does!"

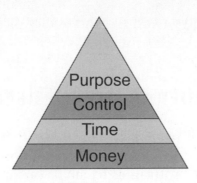

Figure 1.2   The Hierarchy of Freedoms

Thinking his young son was focused and motivated beyond his years, Clate said, "Great, Tanner! What does Jake's dad do?"

"I'm not sure," came the reply. "But he has a ton of money, and he gets to be home all the time."

Tanner's answer provided a rather blunt reality of what most entrepreneurs are looking to achieve. See, Tanner had it mostly right. Money and time are key motivators for driving people toward small business ownership. But they are not the only benefits. Control and fulfillment of purpose are ultimately necessary.

After years of working with entrepreneurs, we realized that freedom, true freedom, is based on a hierarchy of entrepreneurial needs (see Figure 1.2). Understanding the hierarchy will help you realize that money alone doesn't result in long-term freedom. Likewise, if a business owner chooses to take time off, it's not always because he has found his freedom.

MONEY

Whether anyone admits it or not, money itself is one of the most attractive features of owning your own business. For many people, it was the primary reason for leaving the corporate world behind. That's because in the corporate world, people understand that no matter how hard they work or how brilliant they are, the same amount of money will be deposited into their bank account every month. Entrepreneurship, on the other hand, holds the promise of more money, lots more money. It's enough to get otherwise complacent individuals to take action.

That's okay. If there weren't a monetary reward in owning a business, hardly anyone would do it. The financial rewards of success almost *have to* be a part of the equation. It's not greed. It's capitalism. And it's what drives sharp people to solve difficult problems all over the world. Financial rewards, to the entrepreneur, are the grease that makes the whole thing work.

But money can be so elusive. It seems those who have it easily create more of it. Those who don't struggle continually to get it, which is why most entrepreneurs will never get past this level of the hierarchy. They might work for years believing that a little more money would provide them with the freedom they so desperately want to enjoy.

So where does that put you as an entrepreneur? Well, hopefully you're finding some success. Hopefully you have money and are finding ways to easily make more of it. But, while the personal benefits of some extra funds are certainly appealing, once you have money (and you're making more of it), you come to realize that money is no longer the means to the end. It's what keeps a business moving forward.

Has anyone ever told you that "the first million is the hardest to make"? When that concept was first shared with Scott, he laughed. Being young and lacking the experience he has now, Scott always wondered who would need more than a million dollars. You see, he wasn't thinking beyond his immediate desires at the time. As a young man, all he needed was enough money for a house with lots of land and the ability to take vacations with his family.

What he soon realized was money has no stopping point. As long as you hope to stay in business, you will continually need to bring in more sales. So, while your personal bank account may be getting fatter, you'll learn that money itself will not bring you the freedom you deserve. It's a start—a good start—but it is not the cure-all.

In fact, for the first few years of your business, you'll undoubtedly work long, hard hours just to keep the money coming in. Then you'll wish more than anything that you just had a little bit more time.

TIME

Despite the world's dogged pursuit of money, one of life's most valuable, precious commodities is time. Talk to a neighbor, a friend, a family member, and they will all say the same thing, "If only I had more time in my day, I could work wonders." Few individuals (if any) would say they find enough time to accomplish everything they want to do.

We can guess that time was another compelling reason you chose to be an entrepreneur. Chances are good you wanted to develop better relationships with your family. You had a desire to cheer on your son or daughter at a soccer game. You had a "to-do" list a mile long that you were never going to tackle and entrepreneurship seemed to be the answer. You wanted more flexibility in your work schedule so that you would have the time to do things that are important to you.

Yes, before actually starting their own businesses, many people believe that "being your own boss" means *they* get to decide when to work. If they needed an hour or two to watch a pee-wee football game, they could take it. If their family decided to go on vacation, they'd turn the business over to their employees, or simply close up shop for a week. As an entrepreneur, they wouldn't be tied down by a 9-to-5 job.

Small business ownership seems like the perfect solution for someone who knows the only time you'll "find" is the time you make available. But you've already come to realize the chains of time are even heavier when you're the one running the show.

You might bring in thousands, even millions of dollars in sales, but if you have to work 14 to 16 hours a day to make it happen, you're not experiencing freedom. No amount of money can make up for the life you're setting aside to make your business work.

CONTROL

If you were to poll entrepreneurs about why they start their own businesses, we'd be willing to bet that money, time, and a chance to "be their own boss" would be the top three. Why? It all goes back to the factors driving the Entrepreneurial Revolution. People are so disillusioned by the corporate world that they don't want to suffer through it anymore.

In the time you spent working for other people, how often did you think:

"My boss is an idiot."
"If I were in control I would . . ."
"They should just ask me. I know a perfect solution for this problem."
"I would make a much better boss."

As you hear yourself repeat these phrases over and over in your head, it's no wonder you decided not to work for anybody again—except yourself. All of us feel a slight annoyance when *our* ideas, *our* thoughts, *our* suggestions are summarily dismissed. When you start to feel that your value as an employee and an expert in your field is being disregarded, then you want to take matters into your own hands.

The office politics of the corporate world do little to promote the voice of the working class. In an effort to climb the corporate ladder, co-workers infringe on each other's ideas and innovations, managers and directors frequently disregard opinions in favor of their own ideas, and decisions are made by a handful of executives who may be several steps removed from the situation.

For the entrepreneur, docile submission is not an option; and it never should be. You are an innovator. You have the power to create, fill market voids, improve the standard of life for those your business affects, and really make a difference in the world. Who is going to remember the work you did sitting in a cubicle amid hundreds of other workers? No one.

But your family, friends, and even acquaintances will remember you took control of your own circumstances. Rather than complain about your job, you set out to create your own stability and future. No amount of money or time can grant you that satisfaction. Nor can money or time instantly provide you with control. It helps. But all too often, entrepreneurs exchange one boss for another—their business. You'll know you've achieved the control you want when you can do what you want, when you want to. That kind of control is truly liberating.

PURPOSE

Collectively, every other reason for owning a small business can be boiled down to one simple description: purpose. Whether people love what they're doing, want to help a cause, or simply feel a need to create, their "purpose" motivates them to start their own business, and brings them ultimate fulfillment when the business is wildly successful.

Purpose is a tricky thing to describe. It's the one remaining element once your business is growing and you have time, money, and control. After all of that has been achieved, purpose answers the question of "what now?"

For the two of us, this book helps fulfill our purpose. You see, over the years we've developed a real love for small business owners. We've developed long-lasting relationships with our customers and our mentors. But as we've built our relationships, we've seen the pain so many entrepreneurs are going through. We know it doesn't have to be so tough, and our purpose is to help as many as possible avoid the chaos of business ownership.

Your purpose won't be the same as ours. When you reach this level of the hierarchy, you'll know what your purpose is—if you don't know already. Look at successful business owners and you'll nearly always find a philanthropic organization that is established as an offshoot of their company. Even the stingiest business owners will find a purpose beyond the immediate needs of their company or personal life.

That is what the quest for freedom is all about. It's the chance to do more than simply take care of your needs. It's the chance to live life according to your desires, ambitions, and hopes without worrying about your personal circumstances. It's like self-actualization at the top of Maslow's Hierarchy of Needs.

Whatever your purpose may be, you've got to be entirely devoted to it. Because if you haven't learned it already, you will soon discover that even the purest intent is lost once the entrepreneur becomes buried by the business.

It's easy to see how the quest for freedom, as defined by money, time, control, and purpose has led millions of Americans to small business ownership. The Entrepreneurial Revolution is sweeping the country and few are immune to its enticement. But no matter how compelling the end goal may be, most entrepreneurs are not prepared for the reality of small business ownership.

Unfortunately, the Entrepreneurial Revolution will, like all revolutions, have grave casualties. Of the roughly 1,000 small businesses that will be launched today (in the United States alone), most won't be around in three years. And many of those businesses that do survive will struggle mightily.

Revolutions leave casualties. The Entrepreneurial Revolution is no exception to that rule. This book is meant to help you as a small business owner find success so you don't become a casualty to the Entrepreneurial Revolution.

2

ENTER, CHAOS

Chaos in the world brings uneasiness, but it also allows the opportunity for creativity and growth.

—Tom Barrett

So what is chaos? To illustrate what chaos is, we'll use a metaphor we think most people will understand.

A couple of years ago, Clate started going to the gym after years of neglect. When he was young, he ran cross-country. He could go 10 to 15 miles at a time with no problems. But now he was 36. Caught up in life, his body had become—well, let's just say he was no longer the svelte man his wife married 15 years prior. So he bought a gym pass and got a trainer to help him get back into shape.

That first day, Clate was shown around the gym by a slightly arrogant personal trainer. The tour felt a little awkward. Clate already knew how to use the treadmill, the weight machines, and the free weights. The trainer was talking, asking Clate what his personal goals were, and questioning his previous experience with fitness. Clate just wanted to get going. Clate had an image in his head of a stronger, leaner body and he didn't want to delay any longer.

The second day at the gym, Clate arrived ready to work. He could feel his abs getting tighter even as he walked through the front door. But as he looked around, he had to take a minute to get his bearings. Where did he want to start? What did he want to accomplish? Had he really thought about the questions the trainer asked him? Was he ready to take this on?

Deciding to start slowly, Clate chose the most familiar piece of equipment, the treadmill. Taking the pace up to 3.0, he walked for a minute or two, orienting himself, and getting into the flow of the workout. That's when the trainer from the previous day spotted him. Pulling up alongside the machine he said, "Hi, Clate. You planning on going somewhere, or are you just here for a nice stroll?"

Clate laughed at his comment and allowed the trainer to increase the pace. Quickly, this guy doubled Clate's speed to 6.0. It was a good pace. Instead of a light stroll, Clate's legs were moving in a steady jog. His breathing got a little heavier and his body felt warmer, but he remained comfortable.

The entire time Clate jogged, the trainer stayed by his side and talked to him, which was fine. The only problem was that the trainer was increasing the speed of the treadmill. By the time the machine hit 7.2, things were getting tougher and Clate started watching the trainer closely. Again, the trainer reached out and boosted the speed to 7.3.

In a bit of a panic, Clate asked, "How fast are we gonna go?"

"Just want to see what you're made of, Clate."

Okay, wow! What a challenge. Either Clate would continue to run, proving his manhood to this complete stranger, or he would stop. Not one to back down from a challenge, Clate ran, watching every 30 seconds as the speed went up to 7.4, 7.5, 7.6, and onward. The speed was getting faster. Clate was afraid he'd lose his balance and fall off the treadmill. His legs were on fire and his lungs wanted to burst. But in his head, he was stupidly analyzing the situation like this: keep on running, or die of shame.

In the end, Clate was forced to reach up and hit the emergency stop button. He didn't want to, but he also didn't want to end up in a heap on the floor. Bending over and grabbing his knees, Clate gasped for breath. He chugged down the water in his water bottle, grabbed his sides, and walked around to regain control over his body.

The trainer actually laughed at him. "You've got some amazing stamina, my friend."

Days after that experience, Clate continued to feel sore. His muscles tightened up. Standing up seemed almost unbearable, and it was quite a few days before he could bring himself to head back to the gym.

For the entrepreneur, starting a business is like jumping onto a treadmill. You know it's going to take some work, but you can handle it, especially since you're in control of the speed. But here's the problem: Once you've stepped onto that machine, the control is no longer yours. A trainer, bearing the name of "Customer," has just sidled up next to you. And he is increasing the speed on the treadmill whether you like it or not.

In front of you is a fellow gym member who is fit and trim and looks exactly the way you want to look. As he runs on his own treadmill, he teases you with his easy stride and slow, even breathing. That is what you want to achieve. That is the reason you joined the gym, yet this person seems to be taunting you with his perfect fitness.

Still, you can bear the challenge. That is, until another trainer, bearing the name of "Payroll" starts yelling at you from behind, followed by other trainers called "Competition," "Technology," "Compliance," and so on. These trainers are raising the incline of the treadmill, making your workout harder, and reminding you that you *must* keep running if you don't want to die of shame and let down a whole bunch of people.

We could go on and on with this metaphor. But you're in the middle of this; you're fully aware of the chaos you're fighting. And you know what a lonely, difficult fight it is—even though entrepreneurs everywhere are going through the same pains as you.

In the last chapter, we mentioned that only those who have experienced small business ownership will ever be able to understand the chaos that comes from being a small business owner. So, before we get carried away discussing chaos and its effects on the small business owner, we'd like to relate our own story.

Now, we're not sharing our story because we want to go on an ego trip. We are very much aware that we're only two people of the millions of people who go through the business ownership turmoil. Our intent is to give a clear portrayal of the drastic effects of small business ownership, to let you know that living in the chaos has provided us with perspective, and to let you know that there *is* a way to conquer the chaos.

THE INFUSIONSOFT STORY

When we first started Infusionsoft, we really had no idea what we wanted to achieve. All we knew for certain was:

- We had the chance to work for ourselves,
- We were sticking it to the man, and
- Our earning potential was entirely in our own hands, which felt good.

But despite these advantages, it didn't take long before we found ourselves in over our heads and questioning whether we were going to be in business from one month to the next. Naïve as to what was yet to come, we continued to plug away with a glimmer of hope that our budding company would become successful.

The chaos didn't strike all at once. Business ownership seemed exciting at first. We talked about hiring employees, buying our own office space, and acquiring perks and benefits through the business. Our shelves were lined with books that shared the rules for business success. We let ourselves daydream about the life-altering breakthrough we were sure to experience and the financial freedom we were sure to find. We were all working together as close friends. Furthermore, we weren't being tied down by corporate jobs.

But the chaos was steadily changing our reality. Within weeks, the amount of work required to run a small business forced all of us to reevaluate our situation. We began spending more and more time at the office, frequently working through the night just to get projects completed. We forgot the meaning of the term "lunch break." The phrase "9 to 5" dwindled to an ancient and regrettable memory.

It didn't take long before our only option was to eat, sleep, and breathe our business. But worse than the hours put in at the office were the stress and fear that appeared one day and never subsided. These feelings started as a nagging in the back of our minds and soon developed into a full-blown monster raging in our heads.

We were worried about our product, our clients, and whether or not we'd be able to pay our personal mortgages. The carefully avoided question was whether or not we could even make this business work. As if that question wasn't taking its toll, we also developed small business paranoia, the gripping fear that causes business owners to feel the business will crumble to the ground like a house of cards if they step away even for a brief moment. We felt like we couldn't go on vacation, on a date, or to our child's little league game without jeopardizing the business.

Life had suddenly taken on a whole new meaning. Like every new small business owner, we felt trapped, controlled, and consumed by the business. What had happened to the freedom we were seeking? We were propelled into the age-old fight for survival, and the battle wounds were starting to show.

We rarely saw our families, and even when we were around, the business dominated our concentration. We had less patience and little devotion to the people who meant so much to us. Our minds were busy, our stress levels were increasing, and we completely forgot what it meant to live our lives.

Despite the raging personal battles, and almost miraculously, our company progressed, and we hired a few employees to help us manage the work. But, as we expanded, rather

than finding more time, additional business, and helpful solutions, we found ourselves wrapped up in more problems!
Rather than alleviating the chaos, the growth of our company
seemed to be perpetuating it.

For one thing, in order to keep the company moving forward, we needed more money—a lot more money. Making payroll required a lot of cash. We invested our personal
finances into building and growing our company. Multiple
mortgages were taken out on homes. Savings accounts were
pooled. We replied to all those credit card offers and racked
up piles of high-interest personal debt. We leveraged whatever
financial resources we had. Still, it wasn't enough. We were
continually panicked about being able to pay the bills.

On a couple of occasions, we had to approach our employees and explain we couldn't make payroll. To our employees'
credit, they stuck it out and worked hard to help us get through
the tough times. Meanwhile, as the co-founders, we often went
months without seeing any money, or paying any of our personal bills. For a period of about 10 months, we paid our mortgages 30 days late almost every month, because that was the
soonest we had the money to pay it—just in time to avoid a
30-day late rating on our credit reports.

But even as we tried to budget, even as we gave up our own
income, the money continued to run out, and the creditors
continued to come calling.

Clate felt particular embarrassment one night when his
8-year-old son asked, "Dad, why are you so mad?"

"Because a freakin' creditor called me on a Sunday!" Clate
snapped.

The next question was, "What did he want?"

"He wanted to know why I haven't paid my bills."

"Well, Dad, did you tell him it's because you haven't made
enough sales?"

Clate's family all had a good laugh and Clate was glad his
son understood how important sales are to a small business

owner. But that wasn't much solace. The pain we were all feeling was suffocating.

Another time, as Scott sat in the hospital with his wife and brand-new child, he was on the phone, closing a deal. When his irritated wife chided him, he looked down at the newborn baby and said, "You want to be able to afford the hospital bills, right?"

If ever men felt completely overwhelmed and humbled, we were those men. Our *entire lives* were wrapped up in a love/hate relationship with a draining, consuming company. The truth is, there were times when we wanted to get out, but we couldn't because we had so much debt, pride, and fear wrapped up in the business.

We found ourselves struggling to balance our dream and vision for our company with harsh realities. The truth was, without Infusionsoft we had no idea what we were going to do. After a couple of years, we'd invested so much time, money, and effort into the company that failure would have been the ultimate devastation. So every day we trudged through one challenge after another. For the first two and a half years of our business, Infusionsoft was hanging by a very, very thin thread. In terms of our treadmill analogy, the speed was lightning fast and we were so out of balance that we felt a wipeout on the rubber tread was imminent.

Then finally—finally—the clouds started to break, and we knew Infusionsoft was going to be around for a while.

A few favorable circumstances eased the chaos just long enough for us to turn down the speed on the treadmill and achieve a sense of balance. Almost accidental realizations gave us the knowledge to start breaking through the chaos to liberation.

We managed to formulate and perfect our business plan as we went along. We found easier, less time-consuming ways of running the company. We also worked on controlling the chaos in our own heads. Eventually, we moved past the majority of our problems. We were starting to think more clearly and we were starting to recognize there is a better way to run a small business.

Now, as we recount this story, we can smile at the crazy situations we made it through. We can share memories with the loyal employees who stuck with us, and we can laugh together about the funny things that happened back in those days, like the time the two of us took a client to lunch and both forgot our wallets. (He graciously agreed to pay.) Or the time we left the Arizona Farm Bureau Insurance offices after making a software proposal to their marketing director. We walked down to the parking lot, got in Scott's beat-up pickup truck (which was nicer than Clate's beat-up truck which didn't have air conditioning), only to find it needed a push start—twice. Yeah, that was fun to do in the client's parking lot, right beneath the second story conference room with floor-to-ceiling windows where we had just made our software proposal. Talk about humiliating!

But, although we are no longer crammed into a tiny, little office space or driving old, beat-up pickup trucks, we haven't lost touch with where we came from. These experiences intensified our resolve to ease the pains of entrepreneurs who are struggling to grow a business, because it really doesn't have to be so hard.

SYMPTOMS OF CHAOS

Despite the overwhelming power of chaos, no one seems to be telling your story—the true story of the entrepreneur. Unless you are one of the rare overnight success stories, very few people care about the time, energy, passion, and pain you are investing in your business.

New entrepreneurs embrace small business ownership with very little thought about the work and ridiculous devotion a business will claim from them. But it won't be long before they too have experienced all the forms of chaos—physical, mental/emotional, and social—you know so well.

PHYSICAL

For most business owners, it starts with a lack of sleep. As entrepreneurs get more and more involved in their business, they need to find ways to make up for the time they don't have. Although they race all day to get things accomplished, when they fail to meet deadlines or sales numbers, they supplement their schedule by giving up the only time they have left—their nights.

The lack of sleep is soon coupled by an inability to exercise—who has time for that? In our case, we didn't have time to eat, and when we say that we couldn't afford to eat, that's not far off either. Just taking the few extra minutes to fix and eat a meal was time we could use to close a sale or help a customer. Plus, how can you think about eating when your entire schedule is packed with one important task after another?

Now, these are the tangible elements of physical health. Most of us have a clear understanding of what happens to our bodies when we fail to eat and sleep. But, that's only the beginning. The extent of poor physical health goes beyond the basic necessities of eating and sleeping. While your body fights to stay awake (and you load it with caffeine just to get through your day), stress is breaking down all of your physical defenses.

Headaches become commonplace. Immune systems break down. And nagging colds seem to linger. But of course, you've got to work through all of that.

And as if all those symptoms aren't enough, the mental and emotional symptoms move in, reminding us how very human we are.

MENTAL/EMOTIONAL

In addition to running around like a chicken with its head cut off, small business owners are constantly fighting the mental battle of ownership. No matter how good the business plan, no matter how much time you spend preparing for small business ownership, human nature means we continually question our environments and beliefs. So, no matter how certain you might be about your business when you start it, once you find yourself enmeshed in chaos, it's a lot harder to keep believing you're going to survive.

Friends, family and on-lookers question whether you can make the business work. Any time sales decrease, we feel pressure. Are customers also questioning whether we can make the business work? Am I crazy? Do I really know what I'm doing?

When mistakes are made, the ball gets dropped, or customers are unhappy, it's easy to blame yourself, which only adds to the uncertainty and paranoia. In order to make up for the mistakes, lost revenue, or any other things that could go wrong, business owners spend more and more time at the office.

When an employee's performance falls below par, the business owner takes on new frustration. They may feel disappointed, taken advantage of, or even betrayed. As a business owner, you expect the most from your employees, but it won't take long before you come to a truthful conclusion: your employees will never be able to care about your business the way you do.

Through it all, you may start to question whether you, a single person, can really take on all the problems of small business ownership.

But usually, by this time you realize that you can't get out. Even if you wanted to, you are in a position *where you have become the business*. Everything is dependent on you because this is your baby. When we realize no one cares about our business like we do, we allow the business to take over our lives.

When you feel your business is at risk, your life feels at risk. When money runs low or the bills aren't getting paid, the small business owner gets a second mortgage or small business loan to keep things going. After all, giving up on your business is like giving up on yourself. The distance between personal life and business life diminishes to nothing. Not only are lines crossed, there *are* no lines!

We dealt with all of these problems—and not just in the early, uncertain days of the business. Even after the business got off the ground, we felt some of these plagues of business ownership:

- Inability to stop thinking about the business (even when we could sleep)
- Distracted at home
- Mistakes made from the inability to focus on detail
- Lower self-esteem
- No peace of mind
- Desperation
- Depression
- Denial
- Fear

In private, Clate considered getting "a real job," and he strategized how he could pay off his business debt if he walked away from the business. Scott considered purchasing lottery tickets as a feasible way to get out of debt. Furthermore, we completely forgot who we were as people, but our friends and family didn't. And that only made life harder.

SOCIAL

When we started the business, one of the first things we were forced to give up was our relationships. To put it bluntly and embarrassingly, we didn't have time for friends and family. And after a while they didn't have any desire to put up with us.

The first destructive step in the social outlook is the loss of dependability. After you miss a block party here, cancel a golf game there, and repeatedly turn down dinner invitations, friends stop reaching out. Sure, they'll talk to you at church or when you run into each other by chance. But no one wants to invite you anywhere, because chances are you'll either forget or end up canceling.

A good friend of Clate's whom he hadn't seen in years flew in for a single day of conferences. Eager to reestablish ties, this friend called up weeks in advance to let Clate know he was coming. They planned to go to dinner. But the night he came to town, a crisis sprang up. Today, Clate can't remember what kept him from going, but he does remember the disappointment in his friend's voice when he called to say he wouldn't be coming. In speaking with his friend, Clate almost changed his mind. But by then the company had a stronger hold on him than even life-long friendships.

You know, revealing our stories makes us sound like real jerks, but that wasn't the case. We just couldn't think beyond the business. However, we know we're not the only ones who go through situations like this.

The entrepreneur's family members are usually impacted as much as anyone. Think of the impact long hours at the office has on family life. Business owners work all day, deal with unpleasant customers, and are constantly putting out one fire after another. By the time they go home, they're tired, frustrated, and short on patience. Surely you can guess (if you don't already know) what this end-of-day exhaustion does to marriages, parenthood, and other important relationships.

The longer you work in your business, the more distant your relationship with your spouse and children is likely to become. Not that you ever hope or plan to place your family second on your priority list, but they just naturally become so.

Then, we do some weird rationalizing in our heads to the effect that all the hard work we are putting into our business is really to improve the lives of our family. But that's just an excuse to keep running faster on the treadmill. In the meantime, we have families at home wanting their old mom or dad back.

Small business owners everywhere experience the same devastating circumstances. Children and spouses stop trusting and respecting you. When you are home, you might as well be at the office. Without knowing what's happening, your family slowly slips away from you. Oftentimes, small business owners are so ingrained in their business that they don't recognize these unfortunate circumstances. Distrust, resentment, and anger make their way into the relationship.

The good news is that business owners don't have to choose between their business and their family and friends. It *is* possible to grow your business *and* maintain your lifestyle. We'll show you how to do that shortly, but for now just know that it is possible. All you need is the right formula for success. But to understand that formula, you've got to understand where the chaos is coming from.

CAUSES OF CHAOS

It really doesn't matter how you start your business. You could start with piles of money at your disposal, an incredible team of employees, phenomenal mentors, and a bunch of customers lined up to buy your product; or, you could be the entrepreneur with nothing more than an idea. In either case, you are going to experience the chaos. No one escapes it.

So what is the problem? Where does the chaos come from? How does a small business owner find herself gasping for air on a treadmill? Once you understand the answer to this question, you will understand why the formula for success is so powerful.

So let's look at the causes of chaos:

- You're wearing all the hats
- You don't know how to grow
- You are growing—the wrong way
- You're drowning in technology
- You have no central focus

YOU'RE WEARING ALL THE HATS

Think back to when you were working for someone else. Why was it so much easier? Because you had one job to do—just one.

When you become a small business owner, that one job immediately is transformed into 10 or 15 different roles. In addition to selling products or services, managing employees, handling the overhead, and budgeting expenses, small business owners really have little time for anything else. The sad truth is that few business owners are able to spend any time growing and improving their business. Their attention is being constantly pulled in one direction after another, and by the time they have a moment to themselves, they are too drained to do anything more than run the same old gauntlet.

But it doesn't ever stop. Owning a small business doesn't just mean that you have a set number of tasks to do. You never know what's going to creep up next. One day, if the toilets overflow, you'll be forced to add janitor to the roles you take on. (Let us assure you that no matter how in control you might feel, the toilets have a sneaky way of tossing you back into the midst of chaos again.)

Another day, you become a delivery boy. When you fail to meet a customer's needs or a check hasn't been mailed on time, you'll find yourself racing around town getting things where they need to be when they need to be there.

There is no one to back you up. There is only you. If something goes wrong, you have no one to lean on. If you mail out a marketing letter with misspelled words and wrong information, you have only yourself to blame. If you fail to keep solid records, you will be the one giving up your salary to pay additional, unexpected taxes.

Being the entrepreneur means you play *all* the roles in the business—you wear all the hats. (Unless, of course, you hire employees to take on some of those responsibilities. Even then, you'll have more than your fair share of roles to fill. And now you've got to worry about payroll.)

You Don't Know How to Grow

Despite the popularity of entrepreneurship, growing a business is a tremendous fight. You've got to continuously find customers willing to buy your products or services. Plain and simple, without customers, you can't grow a business. You're going to have to pound the pavement to drum up new customers. Meanwhile, your bills still need to be paid.

If you're running the business alone, you are responsible for (1) finding new customers, (2) fulfilling on services for new customers, (3) billing new customers, (4) collecting payments—and the list goes on. That's a lot of work for one person to do. And the worst part is that if you want to grow, you've got to do all this stuff simultaneously. Because if you aren't constantly filling the funnel with new prospects, the pipeline breaks and something or someone (probably you) doesn't get paid.

You Are Growing—The Wrong Way

If you had figured out how to grow your business, you wouldn't be reading this book, right? Not necessarily. Ironically, growing your business the wrong way can actually be more painful than not growing your business at all.

You see, even if sales are flooding in, even if you're making money hand over fist, you can't neglect your other responsibilities. You still have products and services to fulfill, accounting issues need to be addressed, vendors to be paid, employees to be managed, and so on. Though it would certainly be a lot more fun to focus on sales, your time and attention are still required throughout your entire business. But now, with more sales, there are more fulfillment needs, more transactions to track, more products or equipment to be purchased, more required space to work in, and much more chaos!

If you're not prepared for growth—if you haven't got a process in place to manage it—then its arrival is going to demand more of your time and effort. And the result will be that the ball gets dropped, customers get angry, and you'll be running around frantically trying to make everything work. In short, you'll become intimately familiar with the term *growing pains*. So yes, the business may be growing, but you won't be conquering the chaos, and you won't be anywhere close to finding your freedom. Instead, you'll be going crazy!

YOU'RE DROWNING IN TECHNOLOGY

Remember in our discussion of the Entrepreneurial Revolution how we praised the Internet? Well, now we're about to tell you why it's not always our friend. In fact, the same technology that makes it easy to become an entrepreneur can, in many ways, become our arch-enemy. Here are some of the ways.

Data Overload

As great as we think email is, this communication method alone contributes significantly to the chaos. We are constantly bombarded with requests. If we don't have a way of managing the inbox, it will manage us, forcing us into a reactive mode all day long, doing whatever the email senders want us to do instead of doing what will propel our business forward. Email is a big culprit in pushing us from proactive mode to reactive mode.

Social Media Communication

With the Internet technology, communication has increased. Although theoretically, being able to communicate should contribute to your business, in many ways it's too overpowering. Instead of phone calls and letters, we now have to worry about phone calls, letters, emails, faxes, texts, Twitter comments, blog comments, and more.

Too Many Solutions

The Internet has also managed to provide small business owners with too many solutions to their business challenges. That sounds misleading, but companies have developed every possible business "solution," from billing to contact management to email marketing. However, because your business is unique, because no one manages their business quite like you do, how can you possibly be expected to know which solutions will work for you?

Speed

When letters were used as the primary method of communication, business owners had several days of lag time to respond to a customer's request, concern, or situation. Now, a few days is insufficient for making things right. If small business owners fail to respond in a timely manner, they appear to not care. After a while, the entrepreneur is consistently running, running, running just to stay caught up with the most pressing demands.

You Have No Central Focus

In every new beginning there is chaos. Just think of the long list of things the owner of a new business must figure out and put into place before it can run smoothly:

- Organization of a corporation
- Products or services to offer
- Location, office space, equipment
- Marketing strategy
- Sales process
- Customer service and fulfillment
- Employees, payroll and taxes
- Billing, collections and bookkeeping
- Return or refund policies
- Contracts
- Partnerships

In and of themselves, each of those things could take months, even years to perfect. The processes and requirements of each one can amount to thousands of hours of work. But, in most cases, the small business owner alone is responsible for setting up, managing, and maintaining these tasks and responsibilities.

But which one do you start with? Are there some that can be left until later, or do they all have to be done now? Is it more important to focus on making sales once the business is up and running, or should the goal be to create a marketing plan so that business picks up quickly?

For just a moment, think of all the things you were dealing with when you first started your business. It's a wonder that with all the concerns demanding attention in your brain, you were able to make it through the initial stages at all.

No matter how many books you read, no matter how good a business plan you have, the moment you step into business, you've got a million-and-one things that need to be done.

Too often, we hear new small business owners say, "I'll just take it a day at a time." Now, although that philosophy works for different aspects of your life, it's not going to save your business. You can't just take it a day at a time. You need a plan, because in the time it takes you to complete one task, three more are created.

Hard work and endurance will get you far, but it will not get you out of the chaos. Sure, you might experience little wins here and there, but if you're not pressing forward with the *right* kinds of actions, you're not going to see any systematic growth in your business. It will always be the success of a lucky guess. And just how long do you think your luck is going to hold out?

Once a small business owner realizes exactly what the chaos is and what's causing it, there is a tendency to get discouraged. That's because to most people, this situation looks impossible. After years of fighting chaos, even seasoned small business owners resign themselves to the struggle. They come to the conclusion that they can either (1) work in chaos or (2) give up and go back to working for somebody else.

We would say—choose option (3). Conquer the chaos and start living the life you always expected to have as an entrepreneur. We'll show you how.

3

Grow or Die

GROW OR DIE

Growing is the only way to retain any control over your business. You have to fight. There is no maintaining; there is only growing. Without growing your business, the world will pass you by. You must grow or die.

W e're not trying to scare off would-be entrepreneurs when we say: the moment you become a small business owner is the moment chaos moves in. There is not much of a grace period before you start feeling the pressure. No matter what stage you reach in your business, the battle with chaos never subsides. Your only choice is to live with it or find a way to conquer it.

Sadly, most entrepreneurs never find a way to conquer the chaos. Even in the most dire of circumstances, most humans will learn to adapt to their situation. They might be running nonstop for 16 hours a day, but after doing that for months on end, it almost becomes a security blanket. If things aren't out of control, the business owner starts to worry. But when it comes to owning a successful small business, this ability to adapt can be both a benefit and a hindrance.

We're not going to try to fool you. The strategies in this book are not an instant cure-all. They take work. They require that you make real changes in the way you view and run your business. The strategies are not for those who have learned to accept their situation. For those individuals, the best thing we can do is wish them luck and move on.

Our strategies are for the business owner who is ready to break free. They are for the parent who has missed one too many games, the person who is tired of dealing with headaches. They are for the entrepreneur who thinks, "Hey, this isn't what I signed up for. How do I get on the path to freedom?"

Now you may believe that this describes you. After all, you're reading this book. You're ready to conquer the chaos. But before you jump in with both feet, give yourself a moment to really consider the situation. Are you willing to give up what you're doing now to achieve your freedom? For a few weeks, it might mean more work. It's certainly going to take a leap of faith. But most of all, it's a lifestyle change. Your whole mentality has to shift, and that is the greatest barrier for most entrepreneurs.

A MENTALITY OF GROWTH

What you have to realize is that a mentality of growth is the only way you're going to stay in business and find your freedom. To get out of the chaos and find your freedom, you have to grow, period. If you don't believe that, then our strategies are not going to help you. But, if you embrace this idea, we can show you not only how to grow your business, but how you will conquer the chaos through that growth. In other words, you win all the way around, more growth and more freedom!

When it comes right down to it, you don't really have a choice; if you don't grow, you will die. Business is dynamic. It is not static. Every day your business is going to change, and there's nothing you can do about it. The belief that somehow you can maintain your status quo is false.

Your business is being subjected to factors beyond your control. You might be completely satisfied with your current situation, but it won't last. If you choose to stand still, those outside forces will rush past you leaving only chaos in their wake. You see, competitors never behave like you wish they would. Customers have evolving needs. Employees are human and require flexibility, patience and guidance. No matter how firmly you dig in and take root—prepare to be uprooted.

Let's pretend for a moment that you do the same thing every day because you're in maintenance mode not growth mode. What happens?

- Competitors swoop in and take your space
- Employees stop innovating
- Your products quickly become outdated
- You fall behind in technology
- Your income drops

Ultimately, you wind up shutting your doors. The days of reactionary business are over. The best intentions to "ride it out" or stay small are gone. If you want your business to survive, it must be growing. And in its simplest form, growing your business means getting more customers.

In the old days, when there was only one blacksmith in the village, it was safe for the blacksmith to sit back and enjoy his monopoly. He didn't have to market. He could take jobs (or not) depending on his mood. He could charge what he wanted to charge, and the customer didn't have a lot of say in the matter. But as time went on, other factors rode into town and changed the whole game.

First, the blacksmith was subjected to a little competition. Seeing the comfortable lifestyle of the first, another blacksmith came forward and immediately went to work stealing half of the villager's business. It startled the first man, absolutely, but he really had more work than he could handle. A little competition is hardly noticeable.

But what happened when factory-made products made their debut in the village? Suddenly, the demand for the blacksmith decreases. The factory products are better, premade, and a lot cheaper to buy. Now, the blacksmith feels the pressure. In order to stay competitive, he lowers his prices. The lower prices increase business slightly, but now the blacksmith is working twice as hard for the same amount of money. When he's forced to let a few employees go, the workload becomes intolerable for the rest, and they leave.

Before long, the blacksmith is on the road, in search of another village. But no matter how far he travels, the challenges will be the same.

If you're not growing, then you're struggling just to get to tomorrow. But there is no tomorrow. There is only now. Growing is the only way to retain any control over your business. You have to fight. You have to get more customers. There is no maintaining; there is only growing. Without growth, the world will pass you by.

WHY ENTREPRENEURS CHOOSE
NOT TO GROW

We've mentioned that we speak with thousands of entrepreneurs a year. In addition to conversations about chaos, we've spent countless hours discussing the concept of growth. We discovered that those who actively work to grow their companies understand its necessity. These are the same people who are willing to embrace change even when it shakes up their routine. For them, the business is constantly evolving, growing and improving. These individuals are resolute about fighting chaos and controlling their own business.

Those who shy away from growth believe they are saving themselves from additional pain. For them, growth is equivalent to more work, more time and more stress. Their goal is just to maintain an environment they understand. That environment may be one of constant fires and sleepless nights, but it's what they've become accustomed to. For most of these entrepreneurs, chaos controls the business, because the business owner is inadvertently *allowing it* to happen.

Right now, you might be thinking, "Well, I must be in the first category because I'm willing to do whatever it takes to get out of this mess!" But do you really fit that category? Have you fully committed yourself to making the necessary, long-term changes? Are you constantly working to get more customers? Consider the following scenarios carefully because you might be surprised at how well one or two of these situations actually describe you.

SCENARIO #1: YOU DON'T WANT TO GROW YOUR BUSINESS

Sometimes we run into small business owners who insist they *don't* want to grow their business. They have enough customers to keep them busy and keep the bills paid. It's just enough work for them to handle, so they stop trying to build their businesses. They aren't actively looking for new customers. They don't spend any time trying to improve their business processes. They rationalize that the chaos they're experiencing will pass and they believe if they try to grow, they'll simply find themselves in more turmoil.

To us, this is like the ostrich burying its head in the sand to escape from danger.

You cannot hide from chaos. You can't ignore the fact that there are competitors out there just waiting to steal your customers. Even if the work you're bringing in now seems sufficient, it won't stay that way long. Without growing and adding to your customer database, you're putting your business on the line. Your current utopia will slowly fade away as customers turn to your competitors or no longer need you. But we suspect that deep down you already know that.

Plus, we're going to call your bluff. Of course you want to grow. You didn't start your business to become complacent. You started your business to find your freedom. Sitting on the sidelines as the world revolves around you is not going to help you find it. If that's your way of doing things, then the question is not "Will you find your freedom?" but "How fast will you go out of business?"

Saying you don't want to grow is simply another way of saying you don't know how. Well, guess what: Most people don't know how! They're floundering through this just like you. But as long as they're actively pursuing growth, they will be better off than you.

SCENARIO #2: YOU'RE RELYING ON REFERRALS AND REPEAT BUSINESS

One afternoon, a sales representative for a conference we attend called our Event Coordinator. With another conference looming, the sales representative wanted to know if anyone from our office would be attending.

"I don't know," our Event Coordinator replied. "We haven't discussed that."

"Well," came the answer, "When you do figure it out, would you please call me instead of calling the main line? My job kind of depends on the number of people I get signed up. If you call the main line, I don't get credit."

As soon as our employee hung up the phone, she related her conversation and asked, "Am I supposed to be responsible for *her* success? I don't think so. She needs to do her job a little better so she doesn't sound so desperate."

What would be the ideal business situation for you? You have five customers. Each of those five customers tells five of their friends how wonderful your business is. Those 25 friends each tell five more friends and so from referrals alone you have more business than you can possibly handle. Sounds perfect, doesn't it?

But it's not real. Relying on referrals to grow your business for you is a bad idea. You see, like our employee with the phone conversation, even if people like you and your business, they don't feel it's their responsibility to pass on your information. Sure, it might come up in conversation. But people are busy. They have a lot on their minds. They're just not thinking about you.

While looking for his latest house, Scott was handed a business card by a realtor. On the front was the basic information: name, phone number, logo, and so forth. But on the back was one sentence of text that read, "Referrals are the greatest compliment I can receive." Not too long ago, Scott found this card in his desk drawer. Reading the back of the card again he realized that he had not recommended his realtor to any of his friends. And Scott is a small business owner! He knows how important referrals are.

Saying you grow your business through referrals is just another way of saying you don't know how to grow. Don't get us wrong, referrals are great, and you should always be asking for them. But to grow your business and conquer the chaos, you've got to realize the responsibility lies solely on your shoulders.

SCENARIO #3: YOU BELIEVE YOU'LL JUST FIGURE IT OUT

How often do you learn a valuable skill or lesson that could help you in your business but then never apply it? Our biggest fear for the small business owners who read this book is that we'll hand you our strategies for growth and freedom, and you'll never incorporate them in your business.

Millions of people have picked up Michael Gerber's *The E-Myth* over the last 20 years because it's full of some wonderful insights about running a business. One afternoon an employee of ours (and former small business owner) was talking to our marketing director. *The E-Myth* was sitting on the director's desk. This employee picked up the book and said, "I really need to look at that book again. There was some good stuff in there."

Yes! We agree. There is some good stuff in there. But none of it matters if the small business owner refuses to learn from it and then go out and improve his business. As business owners, we get so caught up in the business that we don't take the time to learn from other people. Because by nature we are innovative and motivated, we sometimes prefer to just "figure it out." Undoubtedly you are a smart, resourceful individual; otherwise you would not have accomplished this much. More time, money and control should be just within your grasp, right?

Well, that's where chaos comes into play and messes it all up. See, once you have a company in place, chaos has a powerful way of withholding freedom from the entrepreneur; no matter how skilled, experienced, or hardworking. So, unless you have unlocked your own secrets to growth and freedom, you've got to realize that advice from successful entrepreneurs is invaluable to you and your business.

You can spend the next 10 years figuring things out on your own, battling chaos the whole way. Or, you can take a short-cut by relying on the experiences of those who have gone before you.

SCENARIO #4: YOU DO EVERYTHING YOURSELF—MANUALLY

There are many more scenarios that keep entrepreneurs from achieving their freedom but we want to finish with one last, critical misconception. This scenario is not only the biggest challenge facing small business owners, but the answer to this challenge is an important component of our strategies.

As an entrepreneur, you tend to do everything. In a single day, you might:

- Read and respond to emails
- Check your inventory or schedule
- Design a flier or email to send out to past customers
- Help customers on the phone or in the shop
- Fulfill on the orders that come through
- Enter the sales into Quickbooks
- Clean the store
- Have one-on-one chats with your employees
- And thousands of other tasks

Now we've got two questions for you:

1. How do you determine what things (out of thousands) you will do in a day?
2. Why are you doing all of them?

Ask any entrepreneur and they will tell you there is little predictability in a typical day. Although they may start with a to-do list, by the time they close up shop, the to-do list has long since been disregarded.

Most business owners do not have a system for growth. The tasks they attempt to complete each day are largely random and reactive. One entrepreneur might just as easily spend an afternoon looking at inventory as pick out new tile for their storefront. One day they choose to focus their attentions on marketing, but then they might wait an entire month before doing it again.

If this is the way you do things in your business—stop! If you have any intention of ever finding more time, money, control and purpose, then you need a systematic growth engine. Without one, you're just running on the treadmill, faster and faster, with no real purpose.

INTRODUCING—THE STRATEGIES FOR CONQUERING CHAOS

These strategies are proven methods for conquering chaos, growing your business and finding your freedom. They have been used by us and by thousands of contented entrepreneurs. When you use these strategies you will find renewed ambition and the ability to transform your business into the successful endeavor you always believed it to be.

We've broken the strategies down into two sections: Mindset and Systems. A few notes before introducing these two types of strategies:

- Although the Mindset strategies appear first in the book, this is not meant to suggest you should fully implement the Mindset strategies before implementing the Systems strategies;
- The Mindset strategies build upon each other and the Systems strategies build upon each other; and
- As you implement the Mindset strategies, your capacity to implement the Systems strategies will increase.

MINDSET STRATEGIES

These strategies provide you with balance on the treadmill of chaos. You see, as you fight to conquer chaos, business elements will always be lurking, constantly threatening to defeat you. That's why you must find a sense of balance. You must give yourself the balance and the strength to make your business ownership workout feel like a walk in the park.

Mindset strategies are your preparation for owning, managing, and controlling your business. They give you the power to "refuel" when you feel like you're out of steam. They give you the strength to take control when you feel control slipping from your grasp. They give you the capacity to grow your business without getting consumed by it.

That will happen if you're not careful. At times you will find yourself slipping into old patterns and behaviors. Without adopting these Mindset strategies (and cementing them in your brain), you will find yourself back in the chaos, constantly running *after* your business instead of simply running your business.

SYSTEMS STRATEGIES

Systems strategies are a lot more tangible than Mindset strategies. They are the processes and tools you implement to grow your business and keep it running smoothly and profitably. If the Mindset strategies give you balance, the Systems strategies allow you to control the speed on the treadmill. With Systems strategies, we focus on fixing the flaws in your business that tend to prevent growth and cause chaos.

Systems strategies will teach you about putting the right processes in place to grow your business. In most companies, processes are quickly adopted, but rather than analyze the effectiveness of those processes, small business owners just use them because "that's what they have always done."

The strategies in this book will help you grow your business and stay in control so that you don't feel like you are going crazy. You'll see how to use systems and technology together so that you can grow your business in a smart way, without having to work harder and harder.

Remember, business systems will only get you so far. Your incredible traits as an entrepreneur will only get you so far. You've got to use them together to achieve the four freedoms: Money, Time, Control and Purpose.

In the end, it's really up to you to decide how you will use this information in your business. But think about how much you want to achieve your entrepreneurial dreams. Consider how strenuous the chaos has become. Now, let's get started on Mindset strategy #1: Emotional Capital.

Section II

MINDSET STRATEGIES: ACHIEVING BALANCE

4

EMOTIONAL CAPITAL

If we listened to our intellect, we'd never have a love affair. We'd never have a friendship. We'd never go into business, because we'd be too cynical. Well, that's nonsense. You've got to jump off cliffs all the time and build your wings on the way down.

—Pulitzer Prize–winning author Annie Dillard

W hen new entrepreneurs ask the advice of seasoned business owners, they are sure to hear something like this: "Make sure you have the capital and line of credit you'll need to get the business off the ground." In other words, you need cash.

Of course, that's excellent advice. You'll definitely want the cash to start your business because it will enable you to think clearly. It will also enable you to separate your personal financial decisions from your business financial decisions.

Having said that, we've come to learn that *emotional* capital is even more important than *financial* capital. In fact, your emotional capital, not your balance sheet, is ultimately the strength of your business, which is why it is critical you develop this foundational Mindset strategy. Emotional capital is the currency you use to wake up every day and fight the battle. It's the passion, enthusiasm and positive outlook that propel you through your day, keeping you driven to achieve your goals.

We think it's safe to say that *most* entrepreneurs are able to stay excited about their businesses *most* of the time. But there will be challenges, dark clouds, and curve balls that might knock you unconscious. You can't afford to be knocked out of the game.

Furthermore, the longer you cope with chaos, the more it wears on your ambition and enthusiasm. Many entrepreneurs experience gradual, subtle losses of emotional capital, to the point they go through their work routine in a haphazard, non-committal fashion. This sort of weak emotional approach to the business is certain to produce lackluster results. But when chaos is running rampant and you feel like you're taking on the world, it's easy to let your passion slip. You may not even realize it's happened.

Let's do a spot check right now. Ask yourself if you're "on fire" in your business like you were the day you started it. Ask yourself if you've fallen into the trap of "going through the motions." Ask yourself if you get easily disappointed. Most importantly, ask yourself if you get easily de-focused from your goal of achieving long-term success. If you haven't got a clear picture of what success looks like for you in three to five years, that's a good indicator your emotional capital is not where it needs to be.

YOUR EMOTIONAL CAPITAL BANK ACCOUNT

Emotional capital is intangible and sort of hard to wrap your arms around. But similar to a financial bank account, your emotional capital is stored in a depository of positive feelings, and you'll need to withdraw on that account every single day. The difficult part is that the emotional capital account lies inside of you. You can't look online or call your bank to find out your available balance.

There is, however, a simple way to determine the balance in your emotional capital account. Your balance is determined by the way you get out of bed in the morning and the way you go to bed at night. Do you jump out of bed, excited about the new day? Do you get ready for work in the morning, thinking about the opportunities, the challenges and the exciting work ahead of you? Do you hit the sack, eager to work on your business the next day?

Or, do you wake up worried, scared and nervous? Do you go to bed with a knot in your stomach and the dreaded feeling you had when you were a kid on Sunday night, realizing after a fun weekend it was time to go to school the next day?

You need to honestly evaluate your emotional capital account in the morning and at night. The truth is, most people don't pay much attention to this, and that's a shame. Because if you're not careful, you'll find yourself slipping into apathy, or even fear. And those emotions will never propel you out of the chaos and into the success you want. On the other hand, if you honestly evaluate your emotional capital account morning and night, it becomes second nature and you get very good at consciously making deposits into your account.

Before Infusionsoft, Clate thought he knew something about small business success. Growing up, Clate had always worked for small business owners. Deep down he always knew it was his destiny, too. But we would be disingenuous if we didn't share the truth of Clate's own ignorance about how to start a small business.

You see, when he joined Infusionsoft, he was just a few years removed from graduate school. He left school with an economics degree, MBA, and a law degree, so he thought he was set. *Clate figured that with all the formal education he'd received, he was ready to take on anything.* Plus, he had worked for a few years in a startup software company. When Scott approached him with the idea of joining Infusionsoft, the thought of growing a software company was so exciting that Clate didn't take the time to think about his emotional preparation for the challenge.

He jumped right into the mix when the opportunity presented itself. Maybe you did the same thing. Emotional capital is such a fuzzy notion that it's hard to initially analyze our account balance. Plus, we don't know much about the asteroid belt we're about to launch ourselves into, so it's difficult to determine whether we are emotionally prepared.

Truth be told, Clate did not have the emotional capital account balance he needed to get through the pain of those first few years. Nor did he know how to make the deposits into the account that would propel him and the company forward. If Clate had not had friends and family supporting him, he would not have been there when Infusionsoft finally broke through the chaos.

Small business ownership is tough. It's tougher than tough, and if the entrepreneur is not emotionally prepared for the experience with a strong emotional bank account *and* predetermined ways to make deposits into that bank account, then only a miracle will bail him out.

A couple of comments before we talk about the ways to make deposits in your emotional bank account:

- *If you have not yet started your business*, you need to commit right now that you will start your business with a high emotional bank account balance; and you need to commit yourself to constantly make deposits to that account. It's no different than the financial capital you'll need to start and grow the business.
- *If you are already running a business and you are in the chaos*, this may sound like a warning that is coming too late. Although it is important to do this as a preparation for your business, that doesn't mean it's a step you can skip now. We started working on this strategy about two years after we started the business and it made all the difference in the world! It truly was the key to our business surviving. So, don't skip over this or take it lightly. This strategy is foundational for your success. It is critically important that you embrace it. The truth is you need this strategy even more than the entrepreneur in the brand new business. After all, you have been managing in your own way for so long that you might already be running in desperation, obligation or fear. Your emotional capital must

overcome those feelings and prepare you for the next step out of chaos.

Okay, so let's talk about how to make deposits in your emotional capital account so that this currency will be a powerful asset that helps you conquer the chaos and achieve the success you want.

MAKING DEPOSITS IN YOUR EMOTIONAL BANK ACCOUNT

Wouldn't it be nice if our logical and subconscious minds were able to connect just a little bit better? Wouldn't it be great if we could say, "I need to be willing to take risks," or "I know I can do this," and truly believe it?

That's not the way it works. Some days, you are in control of yourself. You feel strong and confident, knowing that nothing will get you down. Other days, it's a fight from the moment you get out of bed in the morning. You might want to give up your entrepreneurial dreams and go back to living a normal life.

Well, chaos has a way of making those challenging days more prevalent. In the early days of Infusionsoft, Scott used to joke that we seemed to have about one good day per month. Over time, we started to have more and more good days. But the growing number of good days we began to experience wasn't just a function of years in business. The fact is, we learned how to invest in our emotional bank account and that made all the difference. We learned to *make* good days instead of *have* good days.

The goal is to turn your logical thoughts into subconscious thoughts. Somehow, you've got to program yourself to believe you will have a great day. You've got to believe that you can *make* it a great day. You've got to feel empowered before you can conquer the chaos. You've got to always be the one *proactively* controlling your mind. Yes, you've got to actively, rather than passively, think your thoughts.

Here are several great ways to make deposits into your emotional capital account, which will enable you to control your mind and conquer the chaos.

INTERVIEW YOURSELF

This is not to say that you should start talking to yourself—although that's not a bad idea (*if* you are verbalizing positive thoughts). But, the first thing you need to do is decide what you really want and why you want it. If that end goal is not clear, if you are not emotionally tied to a specific outcome, then the only emotions you're going to feel are frustration, uncertainty, despair and fear.

When Clate was a teenager, his dad taught him a critically important life lesson. He said:

Thoughts become words.
Words become beliefs.
Beliefs become actions.
Actions become habits.
Habits become your character.
Character becomes your destiny.

(Apparently Clate's dad got this idea from some guy named Ghandi. And it's as true now as it was when Clate heard it as a punk teenager.)

Everything starts with thoughts. So what thoughts are you having? If you're already in business, and you doubt your ability to simplify, improve and grow your business, or if you question the reality of being liberated from your business, then you will never conquer the chaos. Period. You've got to believe and have faith in the outcome first.

So, how do you come to *believe* the right thoughts? You've got to rewire your brain. You must recognize that our thoughts don't and can't just happen reactively. We are the creators of our thoughts. If you want to believe the right thoughts, you must create the right thoughts.

After you proactively create the right thoughts (and in the process, chase away the wrong, reactive thoughts), you must verbalize the good thoughts. This is where the magic of our mind happens: We believe what we say. Remember: *Thoughts* → Words → Beliefs.

As we said, one great way to cultivate the right thoughts is to interview yourself. Ask yourself these questions:

- Why do I want to be an entrepreneur?
- Why do I want to be successful?
- Is my success worth the hard work I put into it?
- What successes have I seen?
- How can I get more of that success so that my business can become what I always envisioned?

Remember, you are the one in control here. If either your logical or subconscious mind answered any of these questions negatively, try again. See the good in things. Work on yourself until these answers are positive, painting a picture of future success for you. Then, once the interview yields positive thoughts, vocalize your thoughts by discussing your answers with trusted friends and family. The more you do this the easier it will become to believe in your success. And the more emotional capital you will have in your bank account.

It's amazing what getting your mind prepared will do for you. Mental strength is the greatest tool you have for starting, running and growing your business. Remember: this emotional capital is more important than financial capital. Without this emotional capital, the money will disappear when times get tough—and times always get tough.

An employee of ours was given a special project to complete. She started the project excited enough, but only two weeks into it, she lost her motivation. Obviously very upset, she told Scott the project was more than she could handle. But it had to be done, and she was the only person who could do it. Scott couldn't just let her off the hook, so he tried a different tactic.

"What about a bonus?" he asked. "Could you find the motivation to do this if we gave you more money?"

The employee said, "It's no good. I'm not motivated by money. I'm motivated by my need to excel, to do exceptional work, and to do something I feel is of value."

"Well," Scott said, "Then do this project because it's yours. Do it because you can and you can do an amazing job with it." He reminded her of her extraordinary abilities and she began to believe she could do it.

Now, this was a big project and Scott had more than one conversation like this with our employee. But each time he reminded her that she could do it, she acknowledged through *words* she could do it, and she went away feeling empowered again. Remember: Thoughts → *Words* → Beliefs.

You have the ability to do the same thing with your mind. Find your motivation. Think about your goal. Then have that same conversation with those same questions every time you lose your emotional willpower.

The sooner you can learn to positively create your own thoughts, the sooner you will be able to take the next steps in your small business. If you're not having positive thoughts around these interview questions, then keep working on it. Try some of the other emotional capital ideas and then come back to this later.

TALK TO OTHER ENTREPRENEURS

One thing we've noticed is that small business owners feel like they have to be innovative, creative and singular in their businesses. Because their product or service is unique, they feel they must find different ways to manage their problems. After all, their problems must be unique, too. This "rugged individualist" mentality can cause entrepreneurs to live in a cocoon.

In reality, most businesses have similar structures. This means they also have similar problems and challenges. All you have to do is find someone who is willing to talk to you. Then learn from it, grow from it, and let yourself be emotionally strengthened by it.

One of the reasons we survived the hard years of chaos was that we had a network of small business owners we talked to on a regular basis. Plus, we were constantly talking to our customers who were themselves business owners. Not a business day went by when we didn't have a chance to listen to another entrepreneur's story.

Most entrepreneurs don't have the same good fortune of talking to other entrepreneurs all day. They are busy putting out fires, making sales and keeping the lights on. As a result, they get wrapped up in their own stories and fail to consider that others are going through the same thing. It's a shame because the benefits that come from putting like minds together and sharing problems and solutions is powerful. It provides perspective, context and insight that can be obtained no other way.

Think about the human tendency to ban together. In high school, the jocks all hang out with the jocks. The smart kids tend to gravitate toward each other. The skaters hang out with other skaters; band students with other band students. Even the shy, quiet kids have shy, quiet friends. So if we are naturally drawn to those with similar traits to ours, then shouldn't entrepreneurs make an effort to hang out with each other?

We need others. If you haven't had the chance to get three or four entrepreneurs together in one room, you're missing out. The ideas, creativity, optimism, and support that can come out of such a meeting are enough to keep anyone's emotional capital account boosted for days. You will find more creativity and motivation from those like you than you will from any other source.

READ BOOKS BY THE EXPERTS

Sometimes it's just not feasible to meet up with other entrepreneurs. After all, it takes time to schedule something, meet at the determined location, and then return to work or home after getting together. Plus, you don't need to do it all the time. On days when you can't or don't want to get together with others, read books by the experts.

When you need extra motivation, or you simply want a new idea so that you can stay excited about your business, seek out a good book.

Several years ago, Clate reread *The E-Myth* by Michael Gerber. He had read it in business school and thought it was interesting, but not hugely impactful at the time because he wasn't running a business. But when Clate reread Michael's book, it hit him like a lightning bolt. He insisted the other founders read the book so they could all discuss it. What resulted was amazing. As a group, the reluctance to read books changed and now we all read regularly. If you read the right stuff, it will make big deposits into your emotional bank account.

To help you along, here is our suggested reading list of books that will help you build your emotional capital. We have a much longer list of books that we give to employees and entrepreneurs who ask, but this list will get you started:

- *The Power of Positive Thinking* by Norman Vincent Peale
- *Think and Grow Rich* by Napoleon Hill
- *The E-Myth* by Michael Gerber
- *Built to Last* by Jim Collins
- *How to Win Friends and Influence People* by Dale Carnegie

A few years ago, Clate began reading six books per quarter. Like you, he didn't have a lot of time to sit around and leisurely read books, so here are a few things he does so that he can read all those books.

- Always reads books on planes
- Frequently reads books in hotel rooms on business travel
- Forces himself to read very fast
- Reads one book at a time
- Finishes the book in one or two sittings

If he doesn't finish the book in one or two sittings, he probably won't finish it. This whole method of reading books requires fast reading. During the summer between Clate's seventh and eighth grade years, his dad taught him a few simple techniques of speed reading that have helped him read fast. Yeah, we can hear you now. You're saying, "Oh, well, if he can speed read, it's easy to read so many books."

Let me tell you a secret: *you* can speed read, too. It's not hard. Like everything else, it just takes practice. Here are a few tips that will enable you to read very quickly.

1. Focus your eyes down the middle of the page. Don't read the left inch of the page or the right inch of the page.
2. Spend more time reading the first and last sentences of a paragraph than you spend reading the middle of the paragraph.
3. Carefully read all of the titles, headings, subheadings and any emphasized material.
4. *Do not* say the words in your mind. This is the biggie. Most people mouth the words they read or mentally mouth the words they read. This is what slows us down.
5. Push yourself to move through the material very quickly. If necessary, move your finger across the lines of the page in a swift, rhythmic pattern.
6. Recognize that your mind is comprehending what you're reading, even though you are not saying the words. This is

the key. You *are* taking in the material. It just takes time to realize it.

7. Practice, practice, practice. Soon you'll be able to devour books.

If you're not willing to commit to the speed reading thing, here are two other suggestions:

1. Buy books on CD; or
2. Buy book summaries from someone like Audio Tech.

Those two techniques don't work well for Clate, but they might for you.

The bottom line is this: Read from the best business books out there. These books will help you tremendously! They will fill your emotional capital account in amazing ways.

SEEK OUT APPLICABLE QUOTES

We love quotes. It's amazing how much meaning can be conveyed in a few short words. It's even more amazing how those same words have the power to keep us moving even when we are hanging on by a thin thread. Throughout the entire Infusionsoft office, we have quotes lining the walls.

We have quotes that remind us to work hard. We have quotes that remind us to dream. We have quotes that remind our sales team to be bold. We have customer quotes, employee quotes, and quotes from our executive team.

If it has something to do with business, you will find a quote about it somewhere on our walls. No matter what specific challenge you are fighting, somewhere there is a perfect quote to get you over the hump and make a deposit in your emotional capital account.

We're suckers for good quotes because they have lifted our spirits so many times. For several years, Clate has put a new "quote-of-the-week" on the glass by the door of his office. His personal assistant assembles the quotes into binders and occasionally he and others will flip through the quote book, just to make a deposit into their emotional capital accounts.

READ INSPIRATIONAL STORIES

Maybe you're not a quote person. Maybe a few words are not enough to keep you motivated. Maybe you're an individual who wants to see action, and more specifically to see the results of that action.

If this is your mode of inspiration, find a few stories of entrepreneurs that you admire. Maybe the stories of Sam Walton or John D. Rockefeller are inspirational to you. Or, maybe it's the stories of everyday entrepreneurs that lift you up. The fact is, as humans, we are drawn to stories. Stories help us to better understand our own nature. They help us to explain the unexplainable. Plus, sometimes they help us to cope when we're overwhelmed or feel too buried in chaos to press forward.

There's an interesting thing about stories. As you look to the stories of others as a place of inspiration, you will start to realize how amazing your own story is. Sometimes, as bogged-down small business owners, we forget to take the time to appreciate our own efforts. We forget to give ourselves credit for the many things we accomplish. But failing to stop and give yourself a pat on the back is only going to make it that much harder to deal with the chaos.

At Infusionsoft, we have a quarterly process where all employees engage in an exercise of pointing out their departmental and the company-wide accomplishments. The lists are reviewed by the Infusionsoft executive team during our quarterly planning. We spend 30 to 60 minutes discussing the accomplishments and adding to them. During one such session, one of our highly accomplished board members sat in on the meeting. After 20 minutes of observing our "accomplishments" session, he said, "Dang! You guys are going to break an arm patting yourselves on the back!"

That's just fine with us. Because when we review accomplishments, we are reviewing our own stories. We have found over and over that this exercise makes a big deposit in each of our emotional capital accounts.

ALLOW YOURSELF TO DREAM

You may have noticed the words entrepreneur and small business owner both being used in this book. If you're not paying close attention, you may assume that we use them interchangeably. Well, you'd be wrong. There is a big difference between being an entrepreneur and being a small business owner.

An entrepreneur is someone who is willing to take a risk. They know they can do it and they work hard to live life on their terms. But more than that, the entrepreneur is someone who sees possibilities in the world around them. They can turn good things into better things. Most of all, they possess big ideas and even bigger dreams.

In other words, the entrepreneur is the creator. She is someone that can make something out of nothing. She is the brainchild and motivation behind a new service, company or product. The entrepreneur is the dreamer. The small business owner is the one responsible for the day-to-day challenge of making that dream come true.

Most individuals will fill both roles. You will be both the creative genius/dreamer and the person responsible for making that dream come true. The problem is, once the chaos takes over, the entrepreneurial spirit is often forced to go on a permanent vacation. The individual is challenged almost beyond his capabilities. Then, as he fights to get things running smoothly in the business, there is no room for the entrepreneur.

In building emotional capital, you must allow the entrepreneur free rein. Let yourself dream. Be willing to let go. Think about the feelings that drove you to start your business in the first place. What did you hope to achieve? How big did you want your company to run? What were you hoping to find in starting and running your own business?

Allow the entrepreneur time to dream and dream big. As a small business owner, you're used to filling all the roles in your company. Just be sure you don't leave out the role of entrepreneur.

REWARD YOURSELF

Rewards are a great way of keeping yourself focused on small accomplishments. Once in a while, when we concentrate our efforts on the final outcome, we get discouraged as we chase after the ideal. Rewarding ourselves along the way can provide you with the emotional strength and reassurance you need to meet the goals you were shooting for.

How do you reward yourself?

That has to be determined on an individual basis. You have a unique business and you will have to come up with your own unique rewards. At Infusionsoft, every quarter we set a bunch of goals. We also set ourselves up with a potential reward for meeting those goals.

One quarter, Infusionsoft's employees got a crushed ice machine in their break room. Another time, they won a free soda machine. Still another time, they were given three-month Netflix subscriptions. Our employees really dug deep to obtain these rewards, and you should feel the same way about your rewards. Rewards can be the factors that keep you going when your emotional capital is low. If you are like most entrepreneurs, the reward of creation is enough. You don't need anything more. But, taking the time to carefully consider an enjoyable activity or item you would like can be enough to drive you forward when you'd like to give up.

Clate will always remember the time he set a goal for the business and attached the reward of a new car for himself if the business hit that goal. We met the goal and Clate got his car. When done right, goals and rewards not only add emotional capital to your account, they also propel your business forward.

SPOT-CHECK YOUR EMOTIONAL CAPITAL

All of the techniques listed in this chapter will build your bank account of emotional capital. But remember that in order to effectively do this, you must spot check your account balance each morning and night. Having a rough time on occasion is perfectly fine. After all, what happens to us each day is not entirely in our control. How we handle what happens *is* in our control; and our capacity to handle things has everything to do with our emotional capital account balance.

This is the first strategy that will enable you to conquer the chaos. It is a powerful Mindset system that will propel you to effectively use the other five strategies. In other words, if you get this strategy right, the rest of the strategies come much more naturally. If you don't get this strategy right, you're going to struggle big time as an entrepreneur.

Whatever else you do, be careful not to dip into a negative account balance.

Warning: We hope you will not succumb to the cynicism and skepticism often lobbed at those who practice the techniques in this chapter. Cynics will say, "This emotional capital garbage is for the birds." But cynics never create anything great. They stand on the sidelines of life, pretending they are smarter than everyone, not emotionally strong enough to commit to the challenge. You are an entrepreneur. You are out to create something great. You can't afford to be cynical. You need to build your emotional capital account so that you can withdraw from it when necessary, conquer the chaos and achieve the success you want. The faster you kick your inner cynic to the curb, the faster you'll succeed as an entrepreneur.

5

DISCIPLINED OPTIMISM

"You must never confuse faith that you will prevail in the end—which you can never afford to lose—with the discipline to confront the most brutal facts of your current reality, whatever they might be."

—Admiral Jim Stockdale

Of all the strategies, this is the one Clate is most excited to share with you. Perhaps it's because the chapter starts with an incredible story. Maybe it's because implementing this strategy was such a big turning point in his personal as well as his business life. Either way, it's a message that many business owners desperately need.

To understand the basis of disciplined optimism, we need to introduce the Stockdale Paradox to you.

The Stockdale Paradox is a term coined by Jim Collins in his book, *Good to Great*. Within the book, Collins talks about Vietnam prisoner of war James Stockdale. In the seven years Stockdale was held by his enemies in the infamous Hanoi Hilton, he was beaten repetitively but refused to succumb to the demands of his captors (even when it meant beating himself to keep from being used as propaganda).

Because of his resistance efforts, Stockdale was eventually removed from other prisoners and held in solitary confinement. When he was released, Stockdale could barely walk or stand up straight. But he went on not only to receive a Medal of Honor, but to serve for many more years in a distinguished Naval career, to become a business man, and eventually run for vice president of the United States alongside presidential candidate Ross Perot.

Collins recorded a conversation he had with Stockdale in his book. The answers Stockdale gave in his interview were so profound that they have stuck with us and inspired us in our business efforts. One of his statements left a particularly significant impression. He said, "I never lost faith in the end of the story, I never doubted not only that I would get out, but also that I would prevail in the end and turn the experience into the defining event of my life, which, in retrospect, I would not trade."

When Collins asked who didn't make it out, Stockdale replied, "Oh, that's easy, the optimists. Oh, they were the ones who said, 'We're going to be out by Christmas.' And Christmas would come, and Christmas would go. Then they'd say, 'We're going to be out by Easter.' And Easter would come, and Easter would go. And then Thanksgiving, and then it would be Christmas again. And they died of a broken heart."

Stockdale then added, "This is a very important lesson. You must never confuse faith that you will prevail in the end—which you can never afford to lose—with the discipline to confront the most brutal facts of your current reality, whatever they might be" (Collins 2001, 84–86).

That is the Stockdale Paradox: Faith you will prevail plus discipline to confront the brutal facts. You are not a prisoner of war. But the pain you suffer as a small business owner is very real. You are not being physically beaten, but we have seen far too many small business owners beaten mentally and emotionally by their inability to keep their business and personal lives running smoothly.

The practice of disciplined optimism adds upon Collins' Stockdale Paradox and applies specifically to small business owners. We'll show you how this works in just a minute.

When Clate's dad first taught him how thoughts lead to words leads to values (see Chapter 4), Clate didn't buy it. He was a skeptical teenager and he just knew there was more to it than that. It turns out that Clate's dad was right that a positive mental attitude is critically important ... and Clate was right that it is not enough.

Sometimes, problems happen, people make you mad or let you down, and forces outside of your control combine against you. You know what? That's okay. Life is tough. However, the way you deal with life and those circumstances as they come can make things more bearable. But that's where blind optimism and disciplined optimism get confused.

A blindly optimistic person waits in anticipation of the sunshine. A disciplined optimist says, "You know what? I don't see the sun. But that doesn't mean it won't come out another day. I am going to deal with this issue, and move on." With that attitude in mind, they manage their problems and wave goodbye to the optimist who is still searching for a ray of sunlight.

How many times in your business have you set yourself up for something great only to be disappointed? Does it break your spirit? Do you fall into a slump? Do you lose confidence in yourself, your product or your business? Or, do you recognize the disappointment for the speed bump that it is, maintain your confidence and go to work removing that speed bump in your path?

If you are going to survive the chaos, and survive it well, you must be prepared to handle all the pain and unpleasantness that comes with running a small business.

THE THREE COMPONENTS OF DISCIPLINED OPTIMISM

So, what are the three components of disciplined optimism? It starts with (1) an undying belief that your small business will achieve the success you have envisioned, while at the same time, (2) confronting the brutal facts of your current reality, and (3) attacking those brutal facts because you *want* to, not because you have to.

There's a lot packed into that three-part statement of disciplined optimism, so let us take a second and explain each component.

AN UNDYING BELIEF IN YOUR VISION

The first component is absolute belief that your business will achieve the success you have always envisioned. But in order to have that belief, you must define what success means to your business. It's amazing to us how many people don't do this. They're toiling away, day after day, without really knowing what they're working toward.

We have found it extremely focusing and liberating to know, state and broadcast a 10-year plan for the business.

If it seems like too much work to define the 10-year plan, that's okay. We suggest you simply chat with a friend for a while about your business and try to tease out a rough idea for your 10-year goal. If even that seems too tough, at least set a 3-year goal.

Once you've decided on your goal—your definition of success for your business—there are a few things you must do to build an undying belief that you will achieve the success you have envisioned.

Publish It

Write it down, post it by your desk, tell others about it, do whatever you have to do to make it real. Revisit your goal constantly. Publishing the goal makes it real. You can't hide from it anymore. And you'll find great confidence swell inside you as you further publish your goal. When you give life to a goal in this way, you begin to believe (remember: Thoughts → Words → *Beliefs*). Publish the *words* that will help you build an undying belief in your goal.

Remember Your Progress

It's so easy to forget where you were just a few weeks or months ago when you're marching on a path to accomplishing your goal. Don't let that happen. Take time to reflect and consider where you were last month, last quarter and last year. Write down your achievements and celebrate your progress. Take special care to remember the challenges you've over-come and the things you learned in those ordeals. The process of remembering will build your confidence and give you more momentum to achieve your goal.

Patiently, Confidently, *Work* at It

We've found that in entrepreneurship, we don't always know exactly *how* things will work out. But we've also found that if we patiently and confidently work toward the goal, somehow it *will* work out. In other words, as entrepreneurs we need to have a little faith that if we keep at it, everything will turn out in the end. When we look back at past achievements, we are amazed at how closely our results reflect our goals, even though there were times along the path when it seemed like the goal was out of reach. Remember that every success looks like a failure when you're halfway through it.

CONFRONT THE FACTS

The second component of disciplined optimism is the need to confront the brutal facts of your current reality. It's impor-tant to recognize that you must address these issues and chal-lenges at the same time you are maintaining an undying belief in your goal. This "brutal facts" component has the effect of balancing your enthusiasm and focusing you on the work to be done.

You know you're correctly dealing with reality when you:

- Refuse to turn a blind eye to the problems facing you and your business.
- Accept that challenges don't magically go away.
- Recognize problems as challenges to be conquered.

- Tenaciously go to work to remove the speed bumps in your path.

Again, you do this while simultaneously maintaining an undying belief that you will achieve your goal. That's the trick. You must not allow the unpleasant aspects of business to break your spirit. It's easy to get upset, discouraged or numb when you deal with the brutal facts. Stay sharp. Stay positive. Stay focused on your ultimate goal and the realization of that goal.

FIND THE *DESIRE* TO TAKE ACTION

Third, you must *attack* the brutal facts and do so, not because you have to, but because you *want* to. When you find yourself wanting to talk with an angry customer or vendor, wanting to fix a process or system or wanting to deal with a shortfall in payroll, you know you're on the right track when it comes to disciplined optimism.

It is this desire to attack the challenges that lie at the heart of disciplined optimism. Your desire to attack is fueled by your undying belief and channeled by your confrontation of the brutal realities. Disciplined optimism requires attention to all three of these components. We have learned it is an art that requires constant practice and builds tremendous value in your business. And we have seen in our business and in the business of thousands of our customers that disciplined optimism is a great catalyst for small business success.

One of the best places to practice disciplined optimism is in the context of a customer complaint. None of us naturally like customer complaints. We love our customers and want them to sing our praises. As entrepreneurs, we genuinely want our products and services to be of value to our customers, not only because happy customers are good for business, but also because we have a deep human desire to do something good with our work.

For these reasons, it really stings when a customer complains to us. We might get defensive, unresponsive, unsympathetic or angry when confronted by a customer. But disciplined optimism tells us this confrontation is simply an opportunity to accelerate our progress toward our goal, which we *will* reach. If we can get to the bottom of the issue, resolve the matter for this customer, *and* prevent future customers from experiencing disappointment, we have made great strides toward our goal.

Now, it's one thing to say this and another thing to practice it. We've all heard that we need to view customer complaints as opportunities to improve, try to turn lemons into lemonade, blah, blah, blah. But doing it is hard—unless you really understand each component of disciplined optimism.

Let us show you how we learned this lesson. A customer called Clate on the phone and complained about our software. Clate listened to her rant for a few minutes. Several times during the conversation, Clate found himself getting a little hot under the collar. But deep down inside, he knew the customer wanted the software to work for her and he wanted the same thing. So, after she simmered down a bit, Clate told her they both wanted the same thing. Clate apologized that it wasn't working and thanked her for bringing it to his attention so that he could make things right for her *and* help future customers avoid the same frustrations.

We've found an apology like this is the magical part of handling customer complaints with disciplined optimism. Customers like to be thanked. They like to be part of the solution. They like to be told so, and they like to know that we, as entrepreneurs, are determined to improve our solutions for them and the rest of our customers.

The interesting part about this experience was that Clate felt confident and excited because he was *attacking* the problem. When it comes to practicing disciplined optimism, confronting the problem and doing something about it dutifully is not enough. We've got to attack it with confidence and enthusiasm, which is exactly what we should feel because we are accelerating the progress toward our goal.

OPPORTUNITIES TO PRACTICE DISCIPLINED OPTIMISM

Before we point out the areas where you can practice disciplined optimism, we'd like you to consider the alternative. What happens when you succumb to the negativity? Your attitude is affected. Your work product suffers. You impact those around you because your employees, customers, friends and family members feed off your attitude. When you go in the tanks, the impact on others is tremendous. You are transferring the emotional distress from the customer to those around you. You are blocking your progress and you are contributing to chaos. Keep that in mind as you battle each day to practice disciplined optimism.

Now, you could seek out opportunities to practice disciplined optimism, or you can wait for them to come. Chances are, you're not going to have to wait long. The opportunity to develop this skill is going to roll around nearly every day and in various situations.

CUSTOMER COMPLAINTS

As we mentioned earlier, customer complaints offer a perfect opportunity to practice disciplined optimism. After practicing this for several years, when we talk to a disappointed customer today, we get on the phone expecting one of three things:

1. We will have a good conversation with the customer, take care of their concerns and improve our relationship with them.
2. The customer will express their concerns, we'll come to a mutual agreement of what must be done and we will go

to work resolving the issue for this customer and future customers. Even if the customer is still frustrated, our attitude of hope and sincerity will leave this person with a powerful, agreeable experience.

3. We will be unable to reach an agreement with the uncompromising customer and we will agree to part ways on different terms. Even though this customer did not realize the benefits of our software solution, he will leave knowing of our commitment and our undying belief that we will accomplish our goals. And just maybe he'll come back to Infusionsoft down the road when he realizes that we can and want to help him.

Cash Shortages

Cash shortages provide another opportunity to practice disciplined optimism. It seems that making payroll can be one of the most discouraging challenges facing an entrepreneur. Recognize the challenge for what it is: it's just a speed bump. Don't turn negative. You can do it. Go to work and make it happen.

Competitive Pressure

Competition is another business reality that screams for the entrepreneur to practice disciplined optimism. All of us live in a competitive environment. When you see a competitor make a move that encroaches on your market, what do you do? Do you fret? Do you obsess over it? Do you figure out a counter move? We've seen many entrepreneurs unduly stress about the perceived competitive threats facing their business.

The reality is that the market is massive. The creative ways to attack the market afford every entrepreneur a way to achieve her goals. All you have to do is get creative. But you certainly won't accomplish that if you become fearful and paralyzed by your competition. Practice disciplined optimism and you will achieve your goals. After all, your success is dependent on *your* actions, not on the actions of your competitors.

MISSED GOALS

Not making your deadlines or goals is something every entrepreneur experiences. But this provides a great opportunity to practice disciplined optimism. You see, if you missed it, you missed it. There's not much you can do except learn from the situation and keep trying. If you give up, then you've let negativity win. We can think of nothing more profound to explain this concept than the old adage: Shoot for the moon; even if you miss, you will land among the stars.

How great is that comment? Not only does it encourage us to be optimistic and push ourselves to achieve, but it also gives us a way to avoid beating ourselves up when we do fall short. Want to know the truth? You're going to fall short. You will have goals that are unmet and deadlines that are pushed back. Sometimes you must recognize that small goals are just milestones on the way to your ultimate vision of success. Don't waste time fretting about setbacks. Get to work! Keep your vision, win the war and don't get too worried about losing a few battles along the way.

You must set goals, but be prepared with backup plans and give yourself a little leeway in case they don't happen. Make sure you set intermediate goals. Now, when we've presented this idea to others, we've received comments like, "If I have a backup plan, doesn't that mean I've already given up? Shouldn't it be all or nothing? It seems to me that giving myself a way out is deciding I'm going to fail before I even try."

That is not the case at all, and here's why: Over 50 percent of what happens in the first few years of your business is outside of your control. With so many unknowns, you've got to be ready. Having a backup plan is just another way to deal with the brutal facts.

LIMITED RESOURCES

One of our favorite experiences with disciplined optimism happened the first time we sought a business loan for Infusionsoft. We were broke. Our credit was hammered as we tried to get the business off the ground. Our credit cards were maxed. We weren't the ideal candidates for a bank loan. But we were only asking for a line of $25k and we both had a home, each with about $30k in equity. Plus, the monthly payment on the loan would be $300 and we were consistently generating about $20k per month in revenue.

We were definitely struggling financially, but we knew we could juggle things as necessary to make the loan payment. The bank didn't see it that way. They turned down the loan application. At first, we were crushed. We had put a lot of hope into getting that loan. After getting over the initial disappointment, we pulled ourselves up off the mat, called the loan officer and asked why we didn't get the loan. He very frankly pointed out that we didn't fit the standard qualifications. We asked more questions and found that we could show a more favorable picture by submitting a schedule of business assets.

With renewed optimism, we refiled the loan application, including the schedule of assets that had a total value of about $25k. But the next time we spoke with the loan officer, it was only to find out we had been denied again. We went home that Friday night pretty discouraged.

Most entrepreneurs would have given up after the second rejection. We didn't. Over the weekend, we reanalyzed the conversations we'd had with our loan officer. We knew there had to be a way of getting approved. We just needed to make a strong enough case.

By the time Monday morning rolled around, we had our sights set on that loan officer. Clate called him up, acknowledged the weakness in our application, pointed out the progress of our company and argued the case for how we would honorably make the loan payment each month. The loan officer stammered. Clate kept talking. Once Clate finished, and following a long pause, the loan officer finally agreed to make the $25k loan.

Through that experience, we learned a valuable lesson about disciplined optimism. We maintained belief in our goal, we dealt with the brutal facts, and we tenaciously, confidently and aggressively attacked the challenge because we *wanted* to.

Since that experience, we have applied for (i.e., argued for) several loans and we've found that in almost every case, "the third time's a charm." But even if we had not been approved for the loan, we would have found ways to make the best of our situation.

Now, these are just a few of the prime opportunities to practice disciplined optimism. Of course the list of pitfalls facing us as business owners is long and scary if we let it be. Don't give into that fear. State and believe your goals, confront the brutal facts, and attack the challenges with desire so that you can achieve your goals.

PRACTICAL WAYS TO CULTIVATE DISCIPLINED OPTIMISM

We've made disciplined optimism an ongoing practice. We've talked with many people about it, taught it to employees, family members, customers and entrepreneurs across the globe. We don't have all the answers about how to apply it, but beyond the three primary components, we've found a bunch of practical, useful techniques to help you in your practice of disciplined optimism:

- Act quickly. Don't brood and dwell on difficult experiences. Go to work right away.

- Rewire your brain. Stop negative thoughts. Replace them with positive thoughts *and* words.
- Remove yourself. Go for a walk. Take a drive. This is a time to rewire your brain.
- Do physical exercise. Somehow, physical exercise is therapy for the brain.
- Read customer testimonials. This does wonders to remind you of the good you're doing.
- Connect with loved ones. Family and friends have a way of providing you great perspective.
- Smile and laugh. These are pure therapy.
- Recite accomplishments. Remembering and publishing progress this way is powerful.
- Be grateful. List all the things you're grateful for. Bet you won't stay annoyed for long!
- Read inspirational books. This will build your confidence and open your mind to solutions.
- Give a compliment. This does wonders for the person you compliment *and* for you.

Finally, have fun. Fun and laughter are a huge part of our culture at Infusionsoft. We are consistently ranked one of the Best Places to Work because we make sure we don't take things too seriously and we consciously use fun as a tool to help us believe in and accomplish our goals.

We and our employees frequently laugh about the early days when the cops showed up at our little office because the neighbor reported strange smells and late-night activity. They actually believed we were running a meth lab!

We roar with laughter when we recall how using the toaster oven caused a power surge that knocked out the computer servers running the software application for our customers. That was in the *early* days.

We can't help but chuckle when we think of the hours we spent deliberating dumb decisions like what color to paint the door frames in our office. Without the power of laughter, we would have never gotten past those first couple of years. Now, they are reminders of where we have been and what we've managed to achieve.

Overall, just believe in what you're doing, know you'll succeed and roll with the punches.

DISCIPLINED OPTIMISM AND PASSION

When you practice disciplined optimism, your passion shines through. Now, we can sit here all day long and tell you that you need to be optimistic. But disciplined optimism is a lot more than just being optimistic. It's about finding passion and enjoyment in what you're doing.

As an entrepreneur, you need to let your passion shine. Passion has an almost magical ability to attract good things to your business and propel you toward your goals. So you want to do all you can to build and project your passion.

Of course, running a business is tiring, time-consuming, and often frustrating. It's not uncommon for the Entrepreneurial Light to burn out. However, if you're not excited about your products or services, no one else is going to be. Who wants to buy products and services even the business owner doesn't care about?

Whatever you have to do, take the time to rekindle the entrepreneurial fire. Reignite your enthusiasm for your customers, products and business. Your customers and prospects are looking for someone to build a relationship with. What they don't want is someone who is quite obviously tired and who only dwells on the negative. In addition to picking yourself up every day, you've got to project confidence and passion to those you interact with each day.

Emotions are so volatile. As human beings we seek out others to teach us how we should feel. Clate learned that lesson as the oldest boy in a family of six kids. Growing up, he was often the babysitter when his parents chose to go out. Sometimes, when it got dark or a thunderstorm passed through, a younger sibling would come to him in fear.

Often Clate was scared, too. It was natural. He was a young kid. But being in charge, he quickly learned to swallow his own worries and reassure the brother or sister that everything was fine. As long as he could maintain a show of confidence, they went away happy and worry-free.

Your customers and prospects are looking for you to do the same thing. They don't want to see the panic in your eyes as you think of the sales that haven't happened or the numerous tasks that must be completed in an unrealistically short amount of time. You've got to be able to immediately summon your optimistic outlook, and you need to constantly remember to be passionate about your business.

You are an entrepreneur. By nature, entrepreneurs are passionate. Despite the chaos you've dealt with, surely that passion is still in you somewhere. Harness it. Couple that passion with your disciplined optimism and you will become a business owner with every reason to believe in the success of your business, and you'll have one heck of a time getting to that success.

Be passionate! Be excited! Love your business, your customers and the simple joys of entrepreneurship. Pass that passion on to your employees and customers, and you'll see a phenomenal difference in the growth and success of your business!

6

ENTREPRENEURIAL INDEPENDENCE

If you know you are right, stay the course even though the whole world seems to be against you and everyone you know questions your judgment. When you prevail— and you eventually will if you stick to the job—they will all tell you that they knew all along you could do it.

—Ralph Waldo Emerson

A s human beings, we all do it. We seek out the approval, opinions and encouragement we need from those we most trust. Few people in this world are confident enough in themselves and in their abilities to consistently act without seeking the advice and opinions of others. We turn to our parents for advice on how to raise our children. We ask our spouse how we should dress, what car we should drive, gifts we should buy for family members. We ask those around us for opinions about our business. And so the voices, both good and bad, start to distract the entrepreneur.

Even when the opinions are not sought after, they will come flying to your ears. As you embrace small business ownership, you will become the talk of the town. Whether you want it or not, everyone is going to share their thoughts with you. In fact, the more successful you become, the more you're likely to get advice from folks who have "been there and done that." The noise can become deafening.

Opinions and advice are great when someone has a different and sometimes more clear perspective than you have. But who knows more about your business than you? Who is more prepared than you to make decisions about what you will do, how you will act, and what your business should look like?

No one. And juggling advice only leads to more chaos. Sorting out the good advice from the bad, making your decisions and confidently moving forward with them is the essence of entrepreneurial independence.

THE ADVICE YOU GET

During his junior year of high school, Scott was attracted to a cute, smart girl who was in several of his classes. Being an immature teenager, he asked his friend about the girl. The friend's advice? Don't go out with her. According to Scott's friend, the girl was too nerdy to date. He thought Scott would be laughed at by their other friends.

Sadly, Scott listened and never asked the girl on a date. A few weeks later, who should come walking down the hall holding hands but his buddy and the girl Scott liked! Scott was the sucker on that one because he listened to an opinion instead of acting on his own beliefs.

We're not saying that everyone who offers you opinions about your company is planning on leading you astray. In most cases, the advice you receive is probably the sincere feedback of a friend or family member who wants to see you succeed. Sometimes the advice you get is spot on. Sometimes you need to seek out advice from those who know better than you do. But even when you *seek* out the advice of friends, experts, or acquaintances, you've got to take every comment you hear with a grain of salt.

ADVICE FROM FRIENDS

Without a doubt, your friends and family are going to take the most interest in what you're doing. They will also be the most vocal. However, they're also the most likely to make comments and give opinions based on their relationship with you rather than a sincere interest in your business efforts.

A couple years ago, there was a business-savvy man who made a killing in the real estate market. In a matter of two years, this man went from practically nothing to owning millions of dollars in real estate. Needless to say, he was ecstatic about his success and so was his wife. They moved into a big home, replaced all their furniture with new things, and bought a couple of nice cars. Considering the amount of money this young man had brought in, the spending wasn't too extravagant.

But within months of moving into his new house, the relationships this man had developed over the years started to change. Those he frequently spent time with avoided him. Family members who had once turned to him for advice were keeping secrets to themselves.

Many who had encouraged his efforts in the beginning whispered about him behind his back. But they didn't whisper quietly enough and the man heard things like:

"I wouldn't buy a big house like this. They don't need anything this big."

"Real estate is risky business. I wouldn't be surprised if he lost it all."

"He was different before he became so successful."

This man was disturbed by the way his friends and family acted around him and he became leery when those friends offered him advice and opinions.

If you've had success in your business, you know exactly what I'm talking about. You understand the change that happens when others start to see you excelling. So any comments that come your way need to be considered carefully because the person giving advice may not have your best interest in mind.

ADVICE FROM EXPERTS

We're huge fans of expert opinions and advice. We've devoured books by experts, attended conferences and hired expensive consultants over the years. Sometimes, the fastest path to success is to learn from others who have been there and done that, and then apply that learning to your business.

Nevertheless, you are the only real expert on your business. No one knows it better than you. The experts don't have insight to the pains and frustrations you are experiencing. They don't know what you've managed to achieve and how you've done it. And they don't possess your unique set of skills, passion and vision. All they can really do is provide you with advice and opinions in the broadest of terms. So soak up what you can from them, and then proceed to make your own decisions. You cannot rely on anyone else to solve your problems for you.

ADVICE FROM ACQUAINTANCES

Neighbors, employees, vendors and other entrepreneurs are people who really care about you, but they may have a different perspective or opinion than you. Here's the key: They don't have to deal with the consequences of decisions you make. And it's possible they have a vested interest in the decisions that are being made. If they are vendors, affiliates or employees, they have their own criteria for wanting the business to be managed in a particular way.

When Clate worked in small businesses as a teenager, he always thought he knew best how things *should* be done. It wasn't until he was running a business himself that he understood some of the decisions his employers made.

Advice can only get you so far. After that, it's up to you to determine how your success will be achieved. You own the business, nobody else. So, in the end, it's only your opinion that matters.

Ah, but self-doubt keeps us from breaking free of the opinions of the world. No matter how strongly you feel about a situation in your business, you're still inclined to listen to the voices that surround you. And those voices can become loud and paralyzing if you're not careful.

FACING THE CHALLENGE OF INDEPENDENCE

We've got to tell you—this is going to be tough. This strategy requires you to take full responsibility for your actions. You can no longer run to your safety nets when things get a little hairy. You decide the fate of your business. And as you navigate difficult decisions you will be tempted to question just about everything you do.

It's not going to feel good the first time someone makes a suggestion and you don't take it. You're not going to like it when they determine you've become a snob because you wouldn't listen to their great advice. We guarantee you'll hate it when you make an error in your business and old friends make comments like, "Well, I told you so."

Ironically, in making choices about your *own* business, you are going to alienate people. But it's for exactly this reason that you must learn to be self-reliant. Even if you want to take everyone's advice, you can't. It's just not possible. But that doesn't stop people from getting hurt feelings.

If you've been married or had kids, you know how this works. As you start to raise the children, your mother or father will give you some good parental advice. "You should put Sara in soccer." Meanwhile, on the other side of the family, your spouse's mother says, "You should put Sara in piano." Then there's Sara who wants nothing more than to be in dance.

If you haven't had the privilege of going through this yet, you'll learn it in your business. Someone's feelings are going to be hurt. It comes out in an accusatory, "I thought you were going to put Sara in piano."

With your family and personal affairs, you learn to walk on eggshells as you manage your relationships. You don't have that luxury when you're trying to grow your business. There isn't always time to be diplomatic and make sure everyone knows you appreciate their advice and opinions. You've just got to do things according to your best judgment and let folks think what they may.

So when can you say that you have finally achieved Entrepreneurial Independence? Well, for most, it's a process, a series of moments when you grow in your independence. But for those struggling to reach independence, and for those who sometimes dabble in independence, we suggest a few actions that will help you achieve entrepreneurial independence.

DEFINE SUCCESS

One of the reasons folks seek additional input is because their objectives are not clear. If you haven't decided the direction you want to take your business in, figure it out. And figure it out fast. Otherwise, the opinions of others will blow you around like a leaf in the wind.

If you do know what success means for you, remind yourself of that fact constantly. You know what you're shooting for. Others do not. You have a dream that needs to be fulfilled and only you (and perhaps your employees) really get it. But if that dream is not defined, you're going to be open to any and all kinds of suggestions. The more defined your success is, the less likely you are to go hunting for, or be persuaded by, the viewpoints of others.

BELIEVE IN YOUR DECISIONS

Here again is something that blocks your progress on the path to entrepreneurial independence. This boils down to one simple thing—don't do anything half-heartedly. Too often, business decisions have to be made based on limited data, before the business owner is ready. So, the owner chooses a course, all the while questioning his own judgment. As you can probably guess, this opens the floodgates to a chaotic mind of self-doubt. Self-doubt leads to seeking approval and advice.

No matter what your decisions must be, no matter how ill-prepared you are to make them, follow through whole-heartedly. Conviction is essential to making things happen. If you don't believe something is going to work, no one else will either. Then, when it fails, we have a tendency to second-guess ourselves.

We think, "Oh I knew that wasn't going to work out. I should have listened to so-and-so who told me . . ."

Of course it won't work out. It's become a self-fulfilling prophecy! If we don't believe in the choice, or we question what we're doing, we are doomed to failure. And not just any failure, this is a failure where self-doubt and loss of confidence will creep in. Then, in the midst of self-doubt, we turn to others for advice once more. Are you starting to see the vicious cycle?

Just remember this: In almost every decision, the success is not a product of the choice you make; rather, it is a product of the way you carry out your choice.

And by the way, who cares if you fail? It's okay to fail. Heck, we're happy to lose some battles because we know we're going to win the war. The only time it's not okay to fail is if you fail because you didn't put everything you had into your efforts. So, make a choice (it can turn out to be the wrong one, that's okay) and put everything you've got behind it. Get your employees on board. Get excited and pursue your course whole-heartedly.

AVOID ARROGANCE

In shutting out the screaming voices of the world, too many entrepreneurs become puffed up in their own opinions. They move far beyond the grounds of confidently trusting themselves. In their minds, they know what's best—and if they have some success, it might be easy to believe they *always* know what's best.

Listen to yourself. Trust yourself. But know that no one is perfect, and you will make mistakes.

Entrepreneurial Independence requires you to strike the safe haven of self-assurance that lies between ignorance and

Figure 6.1

arrogance. When a business owner becomes overconfident and believes too much in the value of his own thoughts, he is setting himself up for failure. Like the blind optimist who doesn't confront the brutal facts of reality, the arrogant entrepreneur can easily lose sight of the many factors contributing to his success and wind up sabotaging himself.

Scott's dad taught him a great lesson along these lines. He taught Scott that in business, a great motto to live by is, "No Fear, No Ego." We have adopted that as a slogan and have found it to be a great guideline as we strive for self-assurance that lies between the dangerous positions of ignorance on one side and arrogance on the other. (See Figure 6.1.)

PRACTICE STANDING ON YOUR OWN FEET

Entrepreneurial Independence is not won in a single battle. It's a war that you must be willing to fight until you come off triumphant. If it's difficult for you to drown out the concerned voices that have been with you since birth, try it with little things first. But as you practice, you may want to bear a few things in mind.

It's Okay to Let Your Beliefs Change

You've had some interesting experiences since you first started your business. You know more about yourself, the business world and human nature. You've had an abrupt education in pain and suffering. You've learned a lot, and it's going to affect the way you think.

That's okay. Human nature is to grow. If, after going through a few years of struggle, your values and relationships change a little, embrace it. Don't make decisions based on what you "used to do." Make the best choices you know how to make today, even if it goes against your previous beliefs.

Clate and his friend enjoyed watching professional basketball on TV. But when players were interviewed, Clate's friend would often become irritated. "Don't you hate it when players thank Jesus for their wins?" he would ask.

At first, Clate agreed, but over time his perspective changed and he thought he could understand why some of the players did it. The next time his friend made the same statement, Clate replied, "You know, it doesn't bother me anymore."

Now he sensed his friend was surprised and even put off by his response. But Clate's objection from years before now seemed cynical in nature. His years as an entrepreneur brought him to understand the thinking behind the athlete's comment. The cynicism was something Clate had given up.

Don't hide from new perspectives. Accept them as an opportunity to grow your business in better, more productive, more insightful ways.

Warning: If you haven't already done so, take some time now to determine which beliefs and values you will hold sacred and which ones are safe to let evolve. Do the same thing for your relationships. In your growth as an entrepreneur, things will change. If you haven't taken the time to decide which values, beliefs and relationships are untouchable, you may lose who you are and what matters most to you. And if you allow that to happen, no amount of success is worth it.

You Can't Avoid Conflict

Don't intentionally offend anyone, and feel free to walk on the egg shells for a little while as you practice standing on your own. But also bear in mind: You can't please everybody even if you want to, and conflicts will arise. That's just part of being an entrepreneur and it shouldn't keep you from exercising your right and responsibility to run your own business. When you deal with others, be kind, but be firm.

Here's an example: Your brother-in-law finds a new building for you to open your office in. It's not the area you would like, so rather than get into a debate about the value of this location, simply say, "That's kind of you for looking. I'm actually searching in another area."

He will have an opinion. He will try to change your mind. That's when you say, "No, thanks. I'm going to keep looking."

End of story. No debate, no discussion. You stood your ground and allowed for differing opinions while staying in control of the decision. Should your brother-in-law take offense, that's his problem, not yours.

You May Need to Sever Emotional Dependencies

As we grow and mature, there are individuals whose opinions and advice we turn to on a regular basis. As children, this role is filled by your parents. As teenagers, it might be your friends. As entrepreneurs, it might be mentors, partners or employees. We all tend to develop safety crutches, people whose advice and support cover everything from our business to our family to our personal affairs.

If you want to continue seeking that support in other areas of your life, fine. But if you require it for your business, you need to get comfortable with disagreement. If you seek validation for your thoughts and find your "safety crutch" disagrees with you, you need to have the courage to make your own decision and stick to it.

THE BENEFITS OF INDEPENDENCE

Becoming independent doesn't mean you're free from mistakes. It doesn't mean all your decisions will be golden. Some of them will; some of them won't. But you're the one driving the bus. You're the one responsible for mistakes . . . and you're also the one responsible for triumphs. Confidently embrace the fact that you are the decision maker.

When you can ignore the noise, you'll find you're in a much better position to conquer the chaos and find your freedom. Here are some of the benefits you'll enjoy.

You Can Keep a Clear Focus

Hearing the advice and thoughts of others can be a distraction. It clutters your mind. With too many opinions swirling around in your head, you're bound to get confused. Sometimes, the very best thing you can do for your business is stick to your thoughts—your own thoughts.

Scott had the chance to assist in a church softball game, where a group of teenage girls were up to bat. Most had never played softball, or even held a bat in their hands. One by one they came to the plate. Each understood the concept of standing beside the plate, but few had learned anything more.

The parents in the stands chuckled as one anxious player stepped up to the plate and stood directly facing the pitcher with the bat slung over her shoulder. When the pitch came, this young girl struck at the ball almost like beating a hammer. Needless to say, she missed the ball but didn't fail to look rather foolish.

"Turn sideways," one parent yelled from the stands.

"Get the bat off your shoulder," came another.

"Keep your eye on the ball," was a third comment.

Each time more advice was shouted at the girl, she attempted to comply. But with voices coming from every direction, she soon became so confused that she was eventually standing over the plate, knees bent, arms up, turning away from the pitcher.

"No, no!" came the cries from the crowd, and the entire process started again. It didn't take long before the girl became so confused, she gave up and headed back to the dugout in frustration. Understanding her confusion, Scott said, "Forget the noise. Just get up there and do your thing."

The girl returned to home plate and faced the pitcher. Only this time, when the pitch came, she managed to at least make contact with the ball and run frantically to first base. No, her first attempt at hitting the ball did not result in a home run, but she hit it, and she got in the game. Had she listened to the conflicting voices of those around her, she would have never made it past that first at-bat.

Developing the skill of listening to yourself will help you keep your eye on the ball and knock it out of the park when the pitch comes. No matter what good advice you might be receiving from those around you, you've got to figure things out for yourself.

This doesn't mean you can't seek out help. You still need to learn from those who can help you. Feel free to give new ideas a little space in your mind, but when the time comes to act, push everything aside and focus on what your gut is telling you.

You Can Act on Instinct

Another benefit of achieving independence is the ability to act on instinct. If you can't focus because of the many opinions swimming in your head, you certainly won't be able to give your subconscious any room. Your ability to act before thinking will be almost completely lost.

Does this sound silly? Why would you ever want to do something on a whim? Isn't that asking for trouble? Yes and no. Yes if you do it all the time. But in the heat of battle, you need to act swiftly, relying on instinct, without having to logically evaluate every little decision.

You may not agree with us, but we strongly believe in acting on instinct. Because of our "instinctive feelings" we knew that we wanted to build Infusionsoft. (A decision we would make again every day of our lives.) Because of instinctive feelings we knew we wanted to marry our wives. (Also decisions we would make again every day of our lives.) Because of instinctive feelings, we've made thousands of swift decisions in our business and personal lives that have turned out to be great moves that didn't necessarily square with the logical pros and cons facing us at the time we made the decisions.

You can call this gut instinct. To some it may be the spiritual side of your being. Whatever you decide to call it, you've got to cultivate it. One of the best ways to cultivate it is to let go of the comments and opinions that come your way every day. What you will find is that you are a lot more passionate about your business. You'll be excited and willing to take risks again. And when you're willing to take risks, you are acting as a true entrepreneur.

Entrepreneurs succeed because they see things that others cannot see. They look at the future and think what can be—not what is. But chaos has a brilliant way of stripping us of that ability. Chaos turns us into business people. It makes living the dream a harsh reality of tasks to complete.

So never disregard the power of your subconscious. Because while you're busy sorting out details of payroll and inventory, your subconscious is at work cultivating your dreams, ambitions and hopes. If you get so tied up in dealing with your reality that you are no longer able to think past the chaos, you'll soon be lost.

YOU CAN START THINKING CREATIVELY

Creativity is another benefit of independence. Our subconscious mind is always working. It never stops. When our minds are clear, new ideas pop into our heads that we had no recollection of having ever thought before. Instinctive or random ideas come from subconscious thought, and they are generally

111

a product of your strongest passions, experiences and beliefs.

Every time you come up against a challenge, you have the chance to push your creativity just a little further. It is when a decision needs to be made, or a problem solved, that creativity is born. And this is the kind of powerful thinking that can lead to game-changing results for you. When you think through your challenges, before seeking advice and opinions, you're developing your creative skills.

If your mind is full of others' opinions, you'll never find your creative groove. Running to others, before giving *yourself* a fair chance, is a great injustice to your business. You may have the answer sitting on the edge of your brain, waiting to be revealed. But unless you have the confidence to look for a solution on your own *first*, you might miss your chance at creative genius.

YOU CAN STRENGTHEN YOUR BUSINESS LEADERSHIP

A final benefit of independence is the leadership strength you will develop. There can only be one leader on a rowing team. Snow sleds have one lead dog. Professional sports teams have a single Head Coach. If you're going to be triumphant, you need to remember to:

- Work as a team with your employees
- Listen to your team members
- Be a real leader

A real leader is one who is able to think clearly and think for themselves. If your business needed someone else to be the thinker, you wouldn't have a business. But you got here. You overcame the opinions of the world to get where you are. Your business needs you. Your employees need you. Your customers need you. You are the backbone of your company and you've got to stand strong and independent in order to fill that role. A great quote comes from a speech by Theodore Roosevelt on April 23, 1910:

> It is not the critic who counts; not the man who points out how the strong man stumbles, or where the doer of deeds could have done them better. The credit belongs to the man who is actually in the arena, whose face is marred by dust and sweat and blood, who strives valiantly; who errs and comes short again and again; because there is not effort without error and shortcomings; but who does actually strive to do the deed; who knows the great enthusiasm, the great devotion, who spends himself in a worthy cause, who at the best knows in the end the triumph of high achievement and who at the worst, if he fails, at least he fails while daring greatly. So that his place shall never be with those cold and timid souls who know neither victory nor defeat. (Theodore Roosevelt Association)

It's only fitting that this chapter is called Entrepreneurial Independence because you have to declare independence for yourself and your business. You've got to look at the world around you and say, "I know what I'm doing. I can handle this." Literally declare your independence.

Those who succeed—and succeed best—are the ones who seek for success inside themselves. Embrace what you are doing and know that you will triumph. Let the world think what it may. You are an entrepreneur, and you were born to succeed!

Section III

SYSTEMS STRATEGIES: CONTROLLING SPEED

7

CENTRALIZE

Information is a source of learning. But unless it is organized, processed, and available to the right people and in the right format for decision making, it is a burden, not a benefit.

—William Pollard

The shift from the Mindset strategies to the Systems strategies may seem rather drastic. In the last three chapters, we focused your energy on conceptual techniques. We showed you how to clear the chaos from your head so you can better tackle the problems at hand.

With the Mindset strategies alone, you can develop a fairly solid game plan for success. Rather than waking up every morning and charging into battle, your actions will be calculated and deliberate. You'll feel calm and confident. That feeling alone is worth its weight in gold. When you can manage the chaos in your head, you can conquer the chaos in your business.

But, as you know, Mindset strategies alone will not conquer the chaos. It's time for us to introduce the Systems strategies. Systems strategies are different from the Mindsets because they concretely apply to your business practices. They are comprised of three specific actions you must implement in your business if you want to find your freedom. Now that you know the value of the *Mindset* strategies, it's time to get started with the first of the *Systems* strategies: centralize.

THE NEED TO CENTRALIZE

As an entrepreneur, you have an especially complicated situation. In addition to keeping up with the tasks in your

119

personal life, you're trying (in many cases single-handedly) to run a business. Corporations have hundreds, even thousands of people to do the same job you're trying to accomplish on your own. You're the boss, the sales team, the marketing department, tech support, customer service and the janitorial staff. That's a lot to take on, and unless you're supernaturally organized, you've got information, reports, records and financial statements everywhere.

That being the case, you've got to centralize all of that information into a single database. It's time to take everything you're doing and condense it into a workable system. It's imperative that you do so, because if you don't, it doesn't matter how great an entrepreneur you are. Chaos will win.

If you read the Introduction, then you know the basis of the "I have pain" story. Several years ago, when we were still a custom software company, we received a call from a man who was frustrated with his business. After speaking to Clate for nearly an hour, the man, Reed Hoisington, commissioned us to build him a system to better manage his prospect and customer data.

For Reed, it was something he'd been searching for desperately. He didn't just wake up one day and think, "Maybe I should improve some of the systems I'm using to run my company." No, Reed was in pain because a "fire" had started in his business that cost him time, money and the trust of his customers and prospects.

As a skilled entrepreneur, Reed was doing a pretty good job of building a customer and prospect list. One day he decided to run a half-off promotion for his prospects to see if he could win their business. So he pulled out all of his contact lists and went to work sending out emails.

Well, in an unfortunate turn of events and because Reed's lists were not centralized in one database, Reed ended up sending the promotion to his customers as well as his prospects.

Suddenly, customers who were previously content with their purchase were calling Reed on the phone, demanding he refund half their money. After all, they had previously paid full price for the same product now being discounted.

Being a business owner yourself, you know how damaging this was to Reed's business. Sure, it was an honest mistake, but try explaining that to the angry customers who felt they had been lied to. No business can afford to make mistakes like these.

Chances are pretty good you can relate to Reed's story. But you don't have to experience a devastating situation like this to understand how a lack of centralization is going to negatively affect your business. Without a firm foundation to build your business on, without a centralized foundation, you will always be putting out fires, losing critical information and making guesses (rather than educated decisions) about what you should be doing next in your business.

See if any of these situations sound familiar to you:

When talking on the phone with a prospect, you jot down a few details on a note pad. Fifteen minutes later you're headed off to a business lunch and the note pad is still sitting there. Maybe you'll get around to doing something with the information, and maybe you won't.

Another day you might attend a conference. Over the course of a single afternoon, it wouldn't be uncommon to exchange business cards with over a dozen individuals. Of course, when you get back to the office you've got things to do. So the business cards get shoved into a drawer until later.

After a while, relying on your notepads, sticky notes, business cards and inboxes is no longer feasible. It's too much to remember, too much to sort through if you ever want to retrieve information. That's when most entrepreneurs exchange one type of chaos for another by purchasing "solutions."

MULTIPLE SYSTEM CHAOS

People know that decentralized systems are a problem. They know it doesn't make sense to rely on a Rolodex or keep months worth of notes in filing cabinets. Technology has given us faster, better methods for managing that information. But the more a business grows, the more "solutions" the small business owner adopts.

The multisystem chaos starts out slowly. As business owners acquire more leads and more customers, they begin to understand the ridiculousness of keeping business cards. They know they can't possibly keep track of everyone's data, so they purchase a contact management system. Now they can keep the names of all their customers and prospects in a single location. Chaos is temporarily put on hold.

A few weeks pass by, and the business owner realizes they'd like to use email to follow up with their contacts. So, they spend 50 or 100 bucks a month to purchase an email marketing system.

Of course, somewhere along the way the business owner has already picked up QuickBooks to speed up their accounting process. But, realizing there is a big online market, this individual now wants to sell their products/services online. So, they spend a little bit more money and get a shopping cart added to their list of "solutions."

Before they know it, the small business owner is committed to more chaos. Because it takes money, time and effort to manage all of the solutions they've bought in to—make money, save time and use less effort. (That's right. And you wonder why you sometimes feel like you are going crazy?) By themselves, these are all good programs. But trying to manage all of these systems at once can be a nightmare.

Scott has a good friend who has an obsession with duct tape. If something is broken, bent, loose, or unstable, out comes the duct tape. This man's house is full of chairs with duct taped legs, torn power cords that have been repaired with tape, remote controls with the batteries taped in because the covers are missing, and an exercise bike with the seat precariously taped back on.

It's comical, right? But entrepreneurs all over the world have pulled out the duct tape and they're trying to make their multiple systems work. Of course, all they're getting in return for their efforts is a new kind of chaos.

Most of the small business owners we speak to are having a tough time managing because they have:

- ACT! or a similar tool for contact management
- Outlook for their email
- An email marketing system
- QuickBooks for their accounting
- Spreadsheets to piece it all together
- Post-it notes with contact information
- Filing cabinets with letters, bills, testimonials, complaints and more
- A physical- and computer-based calendar; and perhaps
- A shopping cart program to manage their e-commerce

Each of these resources is contributing to small business chaos because each one fights a symptom and not the real disease. But by using multiple solutions, all you succeed in doing is building your business on a sandy (i.e., decentralized) foundation.

THE STRUGGLE OF DISJOINTED SYSTEMS

Thirty years ago, software wasn't even an option for most small business owners. When computers were pricey and rarely used, they were more of a cost than a benefit. Now, well, if you haven't got a computer, you're going to find your road paved in uncertainty and manual labor. Computers adapted, software programs appeared.

Of course, with each trend or innovation, a new need is met. Hence the small business "solutions" we've been discussing. But just because something exists doesn't mean it's worth your time or money. As with most things, each of these solutions is easy to buy. So easy, in fact, that entrepreneurs battling chaos, trying to make their businesses work, can make a purchase online and instantly have access to new hope.

Furthermore, most of these systems are fairly inexpensive. When all you're paying is $50 to $100 a month, it's easy to justify the expense, even if all you want to do is check it out. But you know the reality. You get busy. Then, even if the system you purchased is not meeting all of your needs, you force it to work so you can continue to run your business without any interruption. Meanwhile, you're suffering from both the chaos being created and the things you're not getting done in your business as a result.

Now, despite our harsh criticism, we need to clarify that these programs were not created with the intent of contributing to chaos. They work, and they work well. But not for the small business owner who wants to eventually find their freedom. Here's why:

- They're not built to share
- They prevent you from doing what you should
- Communications are impersonal
- Mistakes are made
- You become the central nervous system of your business

THEY'RE NOT BUILT TO SHARE

With the right knowledge, you can do just about anything you want to. But a lack of knowledge is the first problem with using multiple systems. They aren't built to share information with each other. In a sense, they're bank vaults for your databases.

Information goes in easily enough, and you can pull the information out, but you can't transfer the information from one account to another without manually moving it around.

But who has time to import and export data from one system to the other every time they decide they need it?

Nowadays these programs can generally be integrated, if you have some programming knowledge. But you're a small business owner. You're not an information technology (IT) guy. In fact, the word integration might be enough to terrify you. (If that's the case, you can join Clate in that boat.)

So what are your options?

1. You can hire someone and spend a whole lot of money to integrate your systems. However, if anything goes wrong, you'll be investing more money into getting it fixed.
2. You can learn some programming skills. Good luck finding the time to do that.
3. You can deal with disjointed systems.

When Infusionsoft decided to step in and help Reed with his pain, Reed was suffering from 18 different systems! He'd spent a significant amount of time building his databases. He knew how important his contact information was. But despite his best efforts to check and cross check his work, errors were made. All the work and money he'd poured into building his lists was compromised by the lack of system communication.

Had Reed's databases been centralized into one program, he would have known exactly who had purchased his product in the past. He could have easily pulled (and checked) a list of prospects only. As it was, the list he came up with was a compilation of several databases that failed to communicate.

You cannot compartmentalize your databases because they must work so closely together. Why have an email marketing system? So you can send emails, right? But who do you send them to? To the people in your contact database, of course.

How do you know if the people in your contact management want the emails? You need to know their communication history. How do you know if people in your contact management database responded to the email and made a purchase? By looking at your shopping cart.

Without a centralized database that holds all of this important customer information, you're stuck being the middleman between multiple systems. That's multiple system chaos!

They Prevent You from Doing What You Should

Entrepreneurs know they need their database and they know they need to stay in touch with their contacts. They know that with a little bit of communication they'd get more sales. But the disjointed systems mess keeps them from doing it. Just think about the time involved in pulling a list of prospects from a contact management system, importing them into an email marketing system, then sending the email. And that's a relatively "easy" task.

What if you wanted to welcome new customers and thank them for their recent order? You've got to find the orders, compare them with your customer list to see if the purchase came from a new customer or an existing customer, compile the list, import it into your email marketing system and send off the thank you email. Who has the time to do that?

Eventually the business owner just surrenders to the decentralization. This is very common and very costly. The surrender happens when the small business owner has an idea to send a promotion to customers or prospects—after days of putting the task on her to-do list, she scratches her task off the list because assembling the right mailing list was just too hard (because contact info, order info and customer information are spread out in three or more systems). A good idea is wasted and money is left on the table, all because of multiple system chaos.

COMMUNICATIONS ARE IMPERSONAL

If the business owner doesn't surrender via inaction, he surrenders by taking a shotgun approach to his marketing. What is that? Well, it happens when the business owner wants to send a promotion to a targeted segment of his prospects and/or customers. After attempting to pull a targeted list (and failing because the information is spread out everywhere) the business owner considers abandoning the campaign. But this is a great campaign. So what does our ambitious business owner do? He sends *everyone* the campaign, annoying those who didn't want it and jeopardizing his business relationship with nearly everyone on his mailing list.

MISTAKES ARE MADE

Now on occasion, you might get ambitious. When sales slow down or you wake up feeling enthusiastic, you might decide to reconnect with your contacts or send out a promotion.

But what if the promotion was only for customers who had purchased in the last three months, bought product X and lived in California? Could you find those people? Sure. But it's going to take some time and some help from an employee or techie consultant. And you've got to hope beyond hope that the data you spend hours pulling together is accurate.

Any time you are forced to run manual processes (which is what you have to do to bridge your decentralized, incompatible systems), mistakes are going to be made. It's not that you are incompetent or not paying attention to details. It's just that you're human. You can't do everything right all the time.

Plus, you're in a hurry. You have impatient customers and vendors who won't wait for you. In the struggle to get things done, and get them done quickly, accidents happen. Of course, that means you'll be adding to your already impossible workload because you've got to fix the mistake.

You Become the Central Nervous System of Your Business

Without a powerful, centralized system, your brain is the duct tape that holds the entire thing together. Generally, you alone know where your information is and how to pull the right data together when you need it. You know what lists are being kept on spreadsheets, where to find customer contact information, and who you plan to communicate with. This is a terrible state to be in. What if you decide to take a vacation or you're sick? Everything is placed on hold until you return to sort through your databases again.

To build a solid business foundation and get one step further out of the chaos, you've got to centralize your operations.

THE VALUE OF THE RIGHT SYSTEM

Considering the things we've said, you may think we don't believe in small business solutions at all. But that's not the case—we do. In fact, we're going to tell you right now that if you don't have an actual software-based system for centralizing your business information, you've got to get one.

The reason we're so critical of the numerous small business solutions is because they are "point" solutions. They were created to fill one, sometimes two or three, challenges small business owners face. Each one sprang up independently to meet a need or fill a niche, and they served their purpose—in the past.

Fifteen years ago, when many of these tools were invented, no one needed an email marketing system or e-commerce management tool. Big businesses had centralized solutions that cost a fortune. Even medium-sized companies had solutions. But entrepreneurs were left out of the loop.

However, that's simply not true anymore. Now, there are systems that work exclusively for entrepreneurs, providing you with *all* the tools you need to get your databases centralized and manage some of the chaos.

Find one, and put it in place now! Once you are able to centralize your data, running on the chaos treadmill is going to seem almost effortless, and you will be tapping into several levels of freedom.

With a centralized system, you'll find:

1. More time
2. Less stress
3. Greater confidence

MORE TIME

Remember all of those fires you're forced to put out? You know the ones that happen as a result of your mistakes? Well, fires are often a result of decentralized systems. Once you have your business centralized, the fires are going to significantly decrease, saving you a lot of time.

If you are given the chance to really focus on your business, you'll be surprised at how smoothly it will start to run. With a centralized database you will start catching mistakes before they happen. You'll find easier and better ways to deal with fires in the future. When you do find yourself forced to make quick decisions or take care of immediate concerns, you will have the ability to analyze each situation and make the best choices for your business.

Plus, being centralized will help you find, retrieve and use information a whole lot faster. When you know where to find something, you save yourself time in hunting it down. When you need to locate data (perhaps you need a list of all your vendors) it's just a matter of opening your system. Should you forget the last conversation you had with a prospect, head to your database. A good system will store all that information for you.

LESS STRESS

The second benefit of centralization is that it will minimize your stress levels. When your mind doesn't have to be the glue that holds the business together, you will be more calm, less anxious and more stable. This is one of the ways where a Systems strategy (centralize) dramatically increases your capacity to master the Mindset strategies. Remember: Your mind is a very bad database and when you use it that way, you're stressing yourself out and literally stunting your business growth.

When you effectively use a centralized database, you can view all of your important customer information in one place, enabling you to rest assured that nothing is being forgotten. You can see how many people are late on their payments, what communication your office has had with them and what products they've purchased. Once you see it all in front of you, not only will you be less stressed, but your business can be more profitable, effective and simple.

GREATER CONFIDENCE

Confidence is the great enabler of all human beings. We all perform dramatically better when we are confident. It is true of athletes at all competitive levels. It is true of students on an exam. It is true of attorneys in the courtroom, surgeons over the operating tables and politicians on the campaign trail. It's also true of entrepreneurs. When we are confident, we attract success. We solve problems. We concoct ingenious ideas. We get in "the zone." As entrepreneurs, we thrive on confidence.

Centralization provides confidence. With centralization, you can feel confident hitting the send button on an email because you know you've got the right list targeted. You can talk to a customer on the phone, pull up their contact record and know exactly what they purchased, when they purchased it, any promises you made to them, how they heard about you, what challenges they've suffered, what communications they've received and a slew of other important information.

Centralization allows you to operate on a higher level. You know that each day you walk into the office is going to be a productive day, because you're not running around fixing yesterday's problems. And you're not continuously moving forward, leery of the next issue that might blind-side you.

THE PROCESS OF CENTRALIZATION

There is one more aspect of the centralize strategy that we need to cover. You see, you can't be completely centralized simply because you've found a database to replace all those disparate systems. This strategy requires continual diligence. You must also centralize all incoming information, all processes and all interactions in your business.

Several years ago Scott was doing some programming for our software. He thought he had created a command to clear out a table in the database. Unfortunately, that's not what he had done. Once he clicked the wrong button, our entire database was wiped out. All of our stuff including customers, prospects, orders and vendors was lost.

Our company was turned on its head. We wondered how we could possibly recover all of that information. As a team we searched for records high and low, made phone calls to those we remembered numbers for, emailed others and did a pretty good job of piecing everything back together.

Luckily this happened fairly early on. We didn't lose too much information. Had it happened four years later, we can't imagine how painful it would have been. It would have devastated our business.

If you have a recurring revenue model in your business, you understand. But amazingly enough, we shared this story with a few product-based business owners and got little to no reaction from them. They didn't understand why we were so upset. One business owner even said, "Well, you could always find new customers."

It was then that we realized a large portion of entrepreneurs do not understand the value of their databases. They don't have a "customer base," they have a customer graveyard. *They don't realize that the value of their business is based entirely on their database of customer and prospect information.*

They make a sale, they move on. When the list of hot prospects dies down, they seek out new leads, call or email the list, find the hot prospects and start again. There is no database. And therefore, there is no sustainable business.

This is why we're not done with the centralization chapter yet. You must understand completely that the only reason you have a business is because of the patronage of your customers. Which means that the most important variable in your business, that determines your success or failure, is your relationship with your customers and prospects. Without them, you simply don't have a business.

Don't get so caught up in the chaos of managing the back end of your business that you neglect your database. If you want to build that firm foundation, your database should always be your number one priority.

In the "good old days" of entrepreneurship, maintaining a detailed database was not necessary. Most companies stayed in business because they were the only ones around that offered their services or products.

For you, today's entrepreneur, the competition is fierce. Not only are you competing for dominance in your geographical location, but now you're fighting competitors worldwide because of the Internet. Whether it's fair or not, you're in a sea of competition. All around the world businesses are clamoring for the attention of *your* prospects and customers. The more noise there is in the market place, the better your database needs to be.

But although the competition might seem daunting, you have the advantage. You understand the concept of centralization. As you centralize your business and use your system to build long-term relationships with your customers and prospects, you will always have a list of hot prospects who are ready to buy from you. But it's going to require putting the right process in place.

IDENTIFY HOW INFORMATION IS COMING IN

Because they are overwhelmed with chaos, few businesses have a plan for capturing contact information and adding it to their database. They talk to prospects on the phone and leave critical information on sticky notes or note pads. They attend conferences and gather business cards that get shoved into drawers. You remember these, right?

Not knowing how critical a list is, the result is decentralized information, which leads to chaos. Once you understand the value of your prospect and customer lists, and you're determined to centralize your databases, the first thing you need to do is identify all the places you receive information:

- Phone calls
- Business cards
- Email
- Meetings
- Faxes
- Websites
- Shopping carts
- Letters
- Surveys

Some of this stuff can be automated. If you have the right system in place, you can instantly capture leads from your website. All you do is add a form to your website for visitors to fill out. Once they hit the submit button, your system will automatically import those details into new contact records in your database. You never have to touch a thing.

But even with the convenience of technology, you'll gather information that can't be instantaneously uploaded. You'll still meet new contacts face-to-face, get names from business cards and answer phone calls. If you're smart, you have at least half a dozen ways for new contacts to reach you.

Now here's the challenge—find those contact points. You must know exactly how new information is getting to you. Once you've identified sources of information, you can then decide how to get that information into your database.

Determine the Value

At this point we usually get asked, "Is this really necessary? Is it that big of a deal if I don't put someone's contact information into my database? How much will it really hurt my business if I lose someone's information?"

This all stems back to understanding the value of your list. Let's say, hypothetically, that someone chooses not to buy from you today. What are the odds that person will buy from you in the future? We can tell you right now, they're not very good if you never speak to the person again. However, if you collect their data and reach out to them on occasion, well, that's a whole different story.

At Infusionsoft, as long as an individual doesn't directly tell us they don't ever want to be contacted again, we consider them a valuable part of our database. Every time someone hands us their business card, they're handing us a potential sale. Even if deep down we think they won't buy from us, we're not willing to take the risk. The person's information is quickly added to our centralized database—not left in a drawer.

Determine now what the value of a lead is worth to you and then you'll be prepared to take the right actions in your business.

134

MAKE THE INVESTMENT

This is the step where you adjust your business, minimize your chaos, and maximize the output of your company. You've done all of the preliminary work to centralize your business. You've got one, comprehensive system in place. You have a complete view of your databases. You can see everything from prospects, to customers, to orders, to fulfillment. Plus, all this information is working together so that you never have to be the middle man between multiple systems.

But, as we mentioned, you've still got critical data pouring in from all sorts of places in your business. If it can't be automatically collected, you've got to determine a process for capturing that information and getting it into your system.

You might decide:

- To keep all your phones next to computers. Then, when customers or prospects call in, you can pull up their contact records, or create one as they're talking to you.
- To gather all business cards, sticky notes and notepads into one location and then import the data on a Friday afternoon.
- To hire someone for $10 an hour to update your records for you.

Whatever you decide to do—follow through. If you don't have contact information in a centralized database (where you can use it), you are losing money, wasting time and missing out on opportunities to build strong, profitable, long-term relationships with people.

Yes, it takes some time. Yes, it takes some energy. But if you have a centralization process in place, you'll be amazed at how quickly your routine minimizes chaos. Plus, you'll be prepared for the next Systems strategy.

Now, if you only have 10 customers, all of this will require minimal effort. Keeping your information organized is easy.

But if you have a large list, or intend to build the one you've got, you need to get serious about centralization. You need to realize that you can't just trudge your way through it. Because with every month that goes by, the chaos is going to get worse and worse.

So now is the time to move to the next stage of your business. Get the right system. Pull your data together. Centralize, simplify and clear your mind. Don't make the mistake of patching the chaos with solutions that only create a new kind of chaos. Multiple systems just muddy the waters. On the other hand, with centralization comes better clarity, fewer fires, more productivity and the ability to take control of the chaos.

8

FOLLOW-UP

Follow-up is the best fuel for growth; and growth is the sword that slashes through chaos.

As we mentioned earlier, Infusionsoft first started out as a semi-custom software company. However, working with Reed Hoisington changed everything. You see, what we were able to create for Reed was a system for following up with prospects and customers, tracking the communications, organizing prospects and customers into groups and running the whole follow-up function of his business. He was thrilled with what we created for him and he went away very happy.

But then Reed came back. Turns out, he had a bunch of mortgage broker clients who realized what his software was doing for his business—and they wanted it for their businesses. So, we "productized" the software program and provided it to a few dozen mortgage brokers, who began to rave about the product.

Things were going so well with our mortgage broker clients that we moved away from the custom software business and began selling our "follow-up machine" exclusively to mortgage brokers. Clate was doing the selling, talking to prospects, following up with leads, educating people on the benefits of our software and so on—and then something amazing happened.

We began to use the follow-up features of the software in our own sales and marketing efforts. Suddenly, prospects we had never talked to were calling us up saying they were ready to buy. We were having conversations with people who had heard from us several months earlier and had been receiving our follow-ups. *Streams of prospects were literally coming out of the woodwork, calling us. They were eager and ready to buy.*

THE MOST NEGLECTED MARKETING PRINCIPLE

When prospects began calling us, instead of the other way around, we were floored. It was magic. You see, it's not that we were slacking off prior to this moment; in fact we were working like crazy. Every single person in the company was doing more than his or her fair share of work. We were marketing, making phone calls, actively improving our website, asking for referrals, going to conferences, maintaining a centralized database, networking and so on.

Still, nothing, *nothing* even came close to growing our business with the speed and consistency that occurred when we began following up with our customers and prospects.

That was it! That was the missing component of our business. The moment we realized how important follow-up was to our business was the magic moment that accelerated our move out of chaos. The mastery of effective follow-up transformed our business into a multimillion-dollar company and finally gave us the freedom we had dreamed about for so long!

But what's so interesting is that we didn't suddenly come across a deep, dark, hidden secret that entrepreneurs wish they knew. This is a common principle! If you've been in business very long, then you most certainly have been thinking that you need to follow up more effectively.

The only thing that made our discovery unique was this: we tested it and analyzed it and perfected it until we figured out that *consistent follow-up is critical to conquering chaos and finding your freedom.*

To understand our observation, let us ask you a potentially painful question: "Are you consistently and effectively following up with *all* your prospects and customers?"

We have asked literally tens of thousands of entrepreneurs, marketers and successful small businesses this same question. And you know what? 999 times out a 1,000 the answer is a big, painful *no*!

Our guess is that you're no exception to the rule. No matter how well your business is doing right now, so-so, good, or *great*, you know you're leaving a ton of money on the table.

Now let us ask you a less painful question: "What would happen to your business if you consistently and effectively followed up with all your prospects and customers?"

Come to think of it, maybe that question is sort of painful. But just imagine for a second, how much more cold, hard cash you could have stuffed into your personal bank account last year if you had managed to consistently and effectively follow up with your prospects and customers?

When you fail to follow up, you're losing out on incredible opportunities and causing yourself more pain and frustration. You're stunting your growth and prolonging your partnership with chaos.

A struggling loan officer decided to quit his job. He had tried the mortgage business for several months and only closed two small loans. At the mortgage broker's request, the loan officer decided to give the mortgage business one more month.

"Great," the broker said, "Go back to your leads."

"What leads?" came the response.

"You preapproved seven people in your first month. What happened to them?"

The loan officer shrugged his shoulders. "One hadn't found a house yet. Two had some credit issues. One was waiting for her husband to get back from Iraq. And I never heard from the other three."

The mortgage broker said, "Well, it's a start. Give them a call today."

The loan officer stared in horror at his boss and confessed, "I threw their stuff away. I didn't think I would need it."

Contrast that story with one from our sales department. One day, a business owner called us looking for a miracle. He'd been hit hard by the recession and was on the brink of losing his business. After setting him up with our software, an Infusionsoft consultant told him that the first thing he'd want to do was reconnect with his customers and prospects.

Three days later, the consultant received an email. This business owner had reconnected with his contacts by sending out a promotion. In one day he made more money than he had the previous month.

Follow-up works! It absolutely changes everything about your business. And you probably know it. In fact, you're probably feeling some guilt right now as you mentally add up all the customers and prospects who haven't heard from you in months.

But knowing what you *should* be doing doesn't change what you are (or aren't) doing. Feeling guilt over your lack of follow-up won't make your customers and prospects trust you more. They don't know that you'd like to keep in touch with them and just haven't gotten around to it yet.

Hey, we all *know*, deep down inside, that effective follow-up is the key to turning more prospects into paying customers, and to turning good clients into great clients. But we have found that nearly every entrepreneur is guilty of overlooking just *how much* of a difference it makes to his or her business when effective follow-up is in place.

Plain and simple, if you want to get out of chaos, you've got to fix your follow-up failure. Because nothing can compensate for a lack of follow-up.

HOW LACK OF FOLLOW-UP IS CREATING CHAOS

Don't you wish you had so many new customers coming in that you could pick and choose who you wanted to work with and then turn away the rest?

Wouldn't it be great to know you'd never again have to stress about whether you'll reach your sales goals for the month? No more pulling your hair out and biting your nails in front of the spreadsheet, trying to make the numbers work; no more lying awake at night staring up into the dark, trying not to give in to that tight knot of tension in your stomach, hoping and wishing for it all to be somehow okay when you wake up?

Imagine not having to worry about making your payroll or paying that pile of invoices on your desk. Wouldn't it be just incredible to know you have plenty of new business and money coming in, day-in, day-out, as regular and predictable as the tides?

Well, the truth is, you can do this in your business. It's not snake oil, it's not fantasy or fiction, and it's not hype. It's about knowing a few simple statistics about follow-up marketing.

Consider this: Most sales do not close on the first point of contact. In fact:

Only 2 percent of sales close on the first contact
3 percent close on the second contact
4 percent close on the third contact
10 percent close on the fourth contact
81 percent of sales that close, close on or after the fifth contact!
(Source: Sales and Marketing Executives Club of Los Angeles)

So, according to this statistic, keeping in touch with your prospects is critical to closing more deals. Thus it would make sense for a business owner (who wants more than just a 2-3 percent close rate) to stay in contact with their prospects past the fifth point of contact, right?

Well, even if it makes perfect sense to stay in touch, that's not what's happening.

48 percent of businesses quit following up after the first call
24 percent quit following up after the second call
12 percent quit following up after the third call
6 percent quit following up after the fourth call
10 percent quit following up after the fifth call
(Source: Dartnell Corporation)

If 81 percent of prospects buy on or after the fifth contact with a business and only 10 percent of businesses are following up past the fifth contact, guess who's getting all the business? The 10 percent who keep following up!

Do you see the disconnect? When businesses fail to follow up, they fail to capitalize on the opportunity staring them in the face. Instead, they succumb to the chaos of the standard sales cycle.

Let's talk about the sales cycle for just a minute. Though each business offers different products or services, the sales cycle is about the same for each one, in a very general sense. Before you can have a business, you've got to have customers. And in order to get customers, you've got to generate a few leads. This can be done by advertising, buying lists, setting up a website, referrals and so on. Really, the ways of generating leads are nearly limitless.

But what happens next? Once you have your leads, what do you do with them?

Every time you bring in new leads, the leads you get can be divided into three categories:

1. Leads ready *now* (Hot)

2. Leads not ready now but will be ready some day (Warm—these leads are critical to your success)
3. Leads that may never be ready (Cold or Bad Leads)

The problem is, you can't divide the leads into categories because you don't know which leads go into which categories. In most cases, small business owners make a few phone calls, write a few emails, and complete a quick "temperature check" on the leads they've just received.

Sorting out the most interested candidates, business owners and sales reps tend to chase after hot leads, trying to close the deal. But in doing so, they use up most of their available time and tend to neglect all their other customers and prospects.

Now don't think we're criticizing. This behavior is completely understandable. In order to keep a business running, the business owner needs to bring in money. To bring in money, they've got to make sales. So of course the focus is going to be on the prospects most likely to buy, or customers who look as though they might buy again. This is called *cherry picking*.

This is the stage most small businesses are in right now. And it's the same stage most of them will stay. Because once those hot prospects have either purchased or walked away, the cycle starts all over again. The small business owner needs more sales, so he finds more leads, chases after the hot prospects, closes a few deals, then fulfills the orders and starts back at the beginning.

As long as this cycle continues, the treadmill will continue to speed up. You can almost hear the panicked thoughts of the business owner as they close a sale. Rather than rejoice in their success, they're thinking, "Deal closed. Where will I find my next one?" As long as the small business owner is forced to hunt for new, hot leads, they will be unable to free themselves from the chains of their business. They will be running on the treadmill faster and faster, eventually falling flat on their face.

WHY FOLLOW-UP BREAKS DOWN

It's no wonder that follow-up is not a priority. Consider how much time and effort it takes to keep in touch with a single person. Say, for example, you contact a new prospect. Somehow they stumble across your website and they're instantly intrigued. So they call you up. You spend 10 minutes of your precious time talking with this person (hoping to make a sale) and then discover that they're simply not ready to buy yet. No problem. You say you'll follow up with them later.

What are the chances you'll really follow up again? When it comes time to make that second call or send the brochure, you've got a million other things on your plate. You can't possibly spare 10 minutes for this person and 10 minutes for the next. Chances are, they're not ready to buy anyway. So, you put it off for another month.

But what happens at the end of that month? Nothing.

This is not an uncommon story. You know this one. You've got a pile of customers and prospects that you have intended to reach out to for months. Even if it's just a letter or email saying, "Thank you for your purchase," it's all piling up faster than you'll ever be able to dig yourself out of.

But remember this: "People buy when they are ready to buy, not when you are ready to sell." And this means, by definition, you have to be in front of folks when they're ready to buy. In other words, you have to follow up with them—consistently!

If you don't, someone else will land that business.

And guess what? The person who lands the business will be your competitor, who either followed up consistently, or (more likely) got lucky enough to cross paths with your prospect at the right time.

So now, the 10 minutes, 20 minutes, or hour that you spent on the phone trying to close the deal is completely wasted. Your competition came in and pulled the rug right out from under you.

If you're not following up, you're leaving the door wide open for someone to waltz in and steal your lead.

Of course, everyone says they're going to follow up with the other leads *one of these days*, but the fact is, you don't do it.

Or, if you do follow up, you don't do it consistently and effectively because, quite frankly, it's a royal pain in the neck.

As long as you continue to rely on the standard cycle, your follow-up is breaking down in three critical areas.

HOT, NEW LEADS

"Wait a minute," you think, "How can my follow-up be broken with my hot leads? Those are the only individuals I *am* following up with. In fact, I've spent hours talking to them on the phone, shooting them emails, and sending them the information they requested. If there's one area where I have mastered follow-up, it's with my hot prospects."

Sounds convincing enough, but your follow-up with your new prospects is broken ... and here's why: you're spending too much time trying to close a deal. While you chase hot prospect #1, hot prospect #2 is waiting in the wings. If you take too much time on the first prospect, you're bound to lose the second, no matter how excited about your products or services that prospect may be.

Time is money. If you keep a hot prospect waiting for you, chances are good they won't be there when you return. Furthermore, you are *one* person, why are you spending hours of your time closing deals? You have a business to run. But every day you find yourself on the phone talking about the benefits of your products and/or services with a hot lead. In essence, you're spending your time educating a prospect and leading them to the sale instead of just harvesting those that call you up ready to buy this very moment.

We'll show you how to fix this problem later. But let's move on to the next group of neglected individuals.

UNCONVERTED LEADS

According to the standard sales cycle, only the hot prospects will ever receive attention from your business; you will romance those names as long as you need to until you can close the deal. But what happened to all the other names? You know, the names of the people who weren't ready to buy? In most cases, they get tossed into whatever system the business is using (file folders, spreadsheets, etc.). Usually, the intention is to follow up with them later—when the business owner (or disgruntled sales representative) gets some spare time. But when do small business owners ever find extra time?

If you're experiencing follow-up failure, then you don't realize the importance of the names you are basically tossing away. Did you see the statistics? 81 percent of people don't buy until after the fifth contact. So hypothetically, would you rather:

1. Follow up with hot leads today and close 1-2 percent of them; or
2. Follow up with all your leads and close 81 percent of them a little further down the road?

Since most entrepreneurs have what we call tunnel vision (they can only see the sale that might take place right in front of them), they opt for the immediate close. But in doing so, they are leaving lots of money on the table. Instead of tunnel vision, entrepreneurs need to develop funnel vision, recognizing that all prospects are valuable and must be nurtured through the sales funnel in order to maximize sales.

CUSTOMERS

As you busily negotiate sales with your hot prospects, your unconverted prospects are being tossed to the side. But so are your customers.

Here's a tough question: how much do you value your customers? These are people who are keeping you in business.

How do you feel about them? You appreciate them, right? You know that without them, that shark at the end of the treadmill would have devoured you months ago. So you say you appreciate your customers, but what are you doing for them?

In most cases, a customer gets online or goes to a store and makes a purchase. End of story. The purchase is made, the business owner is happy. But how does the customer feel? Appreciated? Respected? Happy they chose that company to do business with?

At the risk of brushing past critical information too quickly, we're going to share this little tidbit of information. The number one reason customers take their business somewhere else is because they feel unappreciated.

They just gave you their hard-earned money and received a product or service in return. But that isn't enough. Not if you ever want them to buy from you again. See, people are a lot more willing to spend money when they feel that you care about them. They want you to say thank you. They're looking for a business that is willing to show them they are valued.

If you don't take the time to send a quick thank-you note, you can give up hoping for that repeat sale. Which leaves you, once again, chasing after new business and turning up the treadmill speed.

THE BENEFITS OF FOLLOW-UP

We want to do a quick calculation. Let's say your company spends $2,000 on marketing programs and is able to generate 100 leads. Of those leads, five people instantly become customers and spend about $300 a month. Over the next 12 months, your company brings in $18,000. That's a decent return on investment (ROI).

Now, what if 20 of those leads will eventually become customers but weren't ready yet? However, you followed up with them until they were. To make this easy, we'll say all 20 warm leads sign up after one year. From your $2,000 marketing effort, you brought in $18,000 in the first year *and* $72,000 later on down the road. But *only* if you follow up with all your leads.

Is it worth it? If you knew that one marketing campaign could generate that much money, would you make an effort to follow up?

Of course you would. Because even if you were to run a marketing campaign every month, you would never bring in the type of money that following up with customers and prospects is going to give you. Heck, even if 5 of the 20 leads end up buying from you, you have doubled your ROI.

It is only through follow-up that you can exponentially grow your business. Furthermore, it's the least expensive way to grow your business. When you rely on the old sales cycle, then you're limited to how many hot leads your efforts bring in. If you want more sales, you need more leads. With follow-up, you not only get the chance to close the hot leads now, but you're building a reserve of leads to close later (without spending a bunch more money).

But follow-up goes way beyond the numbers and the statistics. See, there's something else to consider here—as you follow up with your prospects and customers, you're building a relationship with them.

Relationships are what give *you*, the small business owner, an edge over corporate competitors. As part of corporate disillusionment, consumers have naturally become distrustful. Rather than look at stores and businesses as providers of our needs, we speculate about the "corporate lies" we're most certainly being sold on.

Our whole lives we've been marketed to. We've heard all the stories and all the "facts" about how we can be better, more attractive, more satisfied in our lives. At this point, we just don't believe it. Marketing and advertising have lost a lot of their appeal and impact. We take everything with a grain of salt.

This mentality, the feeling that we are being cheated or lied to, has been further enforced by the use of social media. As information becomes freely, easily and quickly spread through the Internet, the flaws of any business are exposed. Ten years ago, the used car dealer held the "magic" numbers about how much a car was worth. Today, a consumer can jump online, read BlueBook reports, compare prices with competitors and walk into the car dealership fully prepared.

We read reports and blogs online, trusting the opinions of fellow consumers. Because these individuals aren't looking to take your money, but rather "expose the truth," we're much more willing to trust them.

People are also more willing to trust the small business owner who keeps in touch.

Here is one of the advantages we have as entrepreneurs. As you build relationships with your prospects and customers, through effective follow-up, you slowly dispel the fear and suspicion that consumers naturally feel toward businesses.

That is what consumers are craving, no demanding. If you don't supply them with that sense of trust, you're going to find it progressively harder to close deals. And nothing adds to chaos quite like a bank account running low on funds.

Does follow-up seem overwhelming? Probably. Will it be time-consuming? Maybe. (We'll discuss that in a minute.) But you really don't have a choice. If you want to grow your business, you need the benefits that only consistent follow-up can provide. You've got to shift your thinking from being the hunter who chases down leads to becoming the harvester who scoops up the sales.

THE SCIENCE BEHIND EFFECTIVE FOLLOW-UP

We've spoken with thousands of entrepreneurs who have confessed that if they could just figure out how to follow up more consistently with prospects and customers, they would have much more profitable and dependable businesses.

Over 99 percent of small businesses don't properly follow up. Why? Because they don't have a centralized database, they don't have time, they don't realize how valuable it is, and the truth is, they don't know how to follow up!

That's okay, because no one expects you to know how if you haven't been taught!

But what you can do is learn from the best minds in direct response marketing, people like Dan Kennedy, Gary Halbert and Jay Abraham. These people are masters of the direct response marketing profession, and they know how to maximize sales. By applying their direct marketing principles to the mastery of follow-up, our company has helped thousands of entrepreneurs implement effective follow-up in their businesses.

Let's talk about how to apply these direct marketing principles in the discipline of follow-up.

First, you need to understand that a couple of random follow-up phone calls to each lead will help you close more deals, but it's not going to produce big numbers. Plus, it's time-consuming, tedious and discouraging.

Second, you need to realize that the purpose of your follow-up is to endear you to your prospects and customers so that they trust you, like you, and want to do business with you. *What you need to do is shift from being a vendor to becoming an expert.*

To accomplish this shift from vendor to expert, your follow-up must take a combined approach that incorporates these five elements:

1. Segmentation
2. Education
3. Repetition
4. Variety
5. Automation

SEGMENTATION

Not every contact you have is exactly the same. Though many of them have similar characteristics, your contact lists cannot be lumped into one group. As the business owner, you need to make sure you're sending the right message to the right people at the right time. In other words, the messages you send to your customers and prospects should be targeted to their specific needs and wants. Far too many business owners throw all their prospects and customers email addresses together and send out a mass, generic message to everyone on their list. If you want your follow-up to be effective, you've got to craft messages that work for individuals, not entire databases.

EDUCATION

Your follow-up needs to provide valuable information to your prospects and customers. If you're showing up with no value, you'll wear out your welcome fast. You need to communicate that you are an expert on their side and you deserve to be trusted. You'll accomplish this if you provide them with accurate, insightful information. Truth be told, the sales process is confusing and intimidating for your customers. They want to trust you. Give them the information they need and you'll earn their trust. Help them. Serve them. Provide them expert guidance and they'll appreciate you for it.

REPETITION

It's a proven fact that human beings have to hear the same thing over and over before it sinks in. Follow-up is no different. You know your products and services like the back of your hand, but your customers don't "get it" the first time they hear the message. Don't make the mistake of thinking that if a prospect heard your message once, he understood it. Chances are he either didn't hear it or didn't understand it. Tell him again and again and again.

VARIETY

This doesn't mean you vary your message! You need to consistently tell your message, but your follow-up delivery needs variety. To maximize your sales, *you must use multi-step follow-up sequences that incorporate and orchestrate direct mail, phone, email, fax, voice and other media.* Some prospects will respond to your phone call, others to your email or letters, and others to your fax or voice messages. Serious results come when you contact your prospects using multiple methods.

AUTOMATION

The biggest challenge with follow-up is time. Reconnecting with your prospects and customers could take weeks. That's why no one does it. They're trying to do it on their own and failing miserably. Fortunately, follow-up doesn't have to be difficult or time consuming. All you need is the right software program to make follow-up an automated masterpiece. But because automation is the last of the Systems strategies, we'll leave all of that information for the next chapter.

Follow-up does not have to be hard. It does not have to be tricky. But it does need to be done. You've got to find a way to get it done. Whether you hire someone to help you send out letters and emails, or you find a software solution, it doesn't matter. Just do it. Without follow-up systems in place, you don't have stability in your business. What you have is a never-ending search for the next hot prospect. You have chaos.

If you want the freedom to focus on more than the immediate sale, then you need to remember the value of your lists, keep an accurate, centralized database and follow up on a regular basis. In the next chapter, we'll let you know how you can follow up consistently and effectively so you can grow your business without going crazy.

9

AUTOMATE

The first rule of technology used in a business is that automation applied to an efficient operation will magnify the efficiency. The second is that automation applied to an inefficient operation will magnify the inefficiency.

—Bill Gates

Over the last few chapters we've given you a lot of information to digest. We've told you the Mindset strategies are just as important as the Systems strategies. You've seen how centralization is the first step to getting the chaos in your business under control. You know you must follow up with prospects and customers. These are all strategies designed to help you conquer chaos. However, is it possible you're starting to feel overwhelmed?

You're listening to all the things you *should* be doing and you're wondering how you're supposed to do it all. If you wanted more stuff to manage, you'd simply continue to let your normal chaos have free reign.

You might be thinking, "Once I put the book away, I still have fires. What am I supposed to do about the fires? And how can I possibly add centralization, follow-up and the Mindset strategies to what I'm doing now. It's too much!"

You're right. It is too much. So, this chapter is about leveraging technology to do the work for you.

Far too many small business owners are trying to do the work of an army. They believe if they simply work harder, longer and faster they will be able to achieve anything. Often times they can do amazing things on their own. But, at some point, they get sick, or tired, or too stressed to handle anything else in their life.

But long, hard, monotonous work doesn't make any sense. Manual operations are a thing of the past. Maybe ten years ago they were necessary. But now, there are tools, incredible tools, to help you accomplish ten times what you could do on your own. Technology is the key to helping you achieve liberation from your business. Automation is the result of that technology. And the Internet, yes, the facilitator of the Entrepreneurial Revolution, is also the enabler of automation.

Look, it would be great if there were more of you to go around. But there isn't. There is only one you, and you've got a business to run and grow, not to mention a life to live. Why not put your mundane, time-consuming tasks on auto-pilot?

FROM MANUAL TO AUTOMATED

Perhaps if the truth were told, you would admit being unprepared to start a small business. You may have had some idea how to run a company. But until you strike out on your own, you're not thinking about all the steps required to run a legitimate business. Maybe you had no clue how to legally set up a corporation. You may not have been sure how to generate demand for your products or services. There's a chance you've never hired anyone before, leased a building, created a website or dealt with business taxes.

Nevertheless, not knowing the things we just mentioned, many entrepreneurs still go out and buy QuickBooks right away. Within days, they get on Wordpress to create their own websites (or hire someone to do it for them). If they don't have Outlook or some other email program, they get one. These all seem to be standard processes for getting the business underway.

Why do inexperienced small business owners buy these tools? Because they are the established tools of small business ownership. Everybody knows you need those things if you're going to succeed. Ask the new entrepreneur why they bought QuickBooks, and they'll say, "Because I'm not an accountant. I needed something to help me manage my finances."

Well, we're not machines either. But you don't see entrepreneurs seeking out automation systems almost as soon as they get their companies running. And that's a shame. The tools small business owners use are helping them effectively manage the front end and back end of the business, but nearly every business owner is trying to do the stuff in the middle manually. Because they lack the systems to do it, small business owners are manually:

- Handling the sales cycle
- Following up with customers, prospects, vendors and partners
- Calculating their sales information
- Responding to emails, letters, phone calls and other inquiries
- Managing their employees
- Maintaining inventory
- Fulfilling on orders
- Creating marketing pieces

In most cases, they are failing on all counts. Why? For the same reason they buy QuickBooks. They're not accountants. But with QuickBooks, they don't have to be. Unless they are the Entrepreneur Extraordinaire, they're probably not marketers, salespeople, fulfillment specialists or administrative staff either. However, it is only through automated systems (or a whole lot of work) that they can overcome these deficiencies.

Automation is the key factor to saving you time, money and manual labor. But automation also tends to be the one principle that is missing from most small businesses.

If you were to look at every small business in the country, you would find elements of the first five strategies in nearly all of them. Whether it's by design or by necessity, entrepreneurs start to learn the value of those strategies and even implement them to some degree. Only a small percentage ever add automation to their business.

Perhaps it's because automation isn't one of those things you just accidentally stumble upon and learn from experience. Automation is intentional and purposeful and it will propel you out of chaos into liberation. Now let us show you why it is so critical for your success in conquering the chaos.

If you were to show us the to-do list for your day, it would most probably look something like Figure 9.1.

Figure 9.1   To-Do List

If you get any time, you intend to follow up with your customers and prospects. You might plan to put together a new marketing campaign. Perhaps you need to seek out a new method of generating leads. Also, floating in the back of your mind is the nagging feeling that you need to hire a new employee, a process that could take weeks to complete.

Certainly you've got a lot on your plate. But at the risk of re-visiting the pain of chaos, we've got to ask: at the end of the day, how many of those items will be crossed off your list?

If you are an exceptional small business owner, you might accomplish four of them. You'll likely talk to those unhappy customers, check and respond to your email, make a few sales calls and complete one other thing on the list. Ironically, no matter what tomorrow's to-do list looks like, you might: talk to unhappy customers, check and respond to your email, make a few sales calls and complete one other thing on the list.

Why? Because that's all you have time for. You spend most of your efforts trying to close deals and bring in revenue. You're spending hours educating your prospects about your products or services over the phone and through email. Then, when you haven't got enough time to take care of your existing customers, you're forced to handle their needs *after* you've made a mistake and they're irritated.

This is not where you should be spending your time. You are the business owner. You have so much to take care of you can't possibly spend three quarters of your day on four tasks. Besides, the reality is there are a million things you could be doing in your business. There are only a handful that will make you any money. Dealing with cranky customers, educating leads that aren't ready, and picking out tile aren't on the list. So why are you doing it?

We'll tell you why. You're doing it because a business needs money to survive, angry customers will never go away, and sometimes it's more enjoyable to think about tile than to deal with chaos. Unless the business owner can find someone to do this work for them, they must do it themselves, but it's not one of the hats the small business owner should be wearing. As our friend Michael Gerber says, "You should be working ON your business not IN it" (Gerber 1995, 97).

If you can relate to all the things we just shared, then you're too caught up in the chaos. It's time to pass the manual stuff on to someone else. So now you've got two options:

1. Hire someone to take over these responsibilities and live in the same mess you've been dealing with.
2. Get an automated system in place to manage it for you.

Obviously it's better to put a system in place. Hiring employees is important, and as you grow, you're going to have a greater need for them. However, subjecting anyone to the mess you've been dealing with is simply inhuman. Eventually, the person you hire will make mistakes (just like you have), need more help to control the chaos and probably run away screaming. Besides, they won't care the way you do, so they'll make more mistakes than you and you'll spend a bunch of time putting out *their* fires.

What you need is automated software to lighten your load. It's the only way you can keep up. As more demands are placed on your shoulders, you're getting more and more immersed in the chaos. The longer you wait to find an automated solution, the longer it's going to take to get the system working for you.

Like the centralization strategy, you can't personally satisfy the demands of automation. You will have to find a system that automates the business for you. It doesn't matter which automation software you choose, as long as it takes care of your needs. But be careful about the word automation. A rolodex used to be an old-school solution for managing contacts. A contact manager is a digitized Rolodex, but it's not automation. That's just software.

Find a software solution that truly automates your business processes and doesn't just reformat them into a digital state.

You need software that acts and reacts with no or minimal input from you.

WHAT YOU CAN AND *SHOULD* AUTOMATE

Here's a thought: If automation is so effective and as critical to business growth as we say, then why aren't more small businesses adopting automation systems?

Having worked with thousands of small business owners, we have a pretty good idea what keeps people from experiencing the beauty of automation in their businesses.

Automation has been around for a long time. But it doesn't mean small businesses are used to the concept. Automation has long been dominated by the corporate world. Only within the past few years have automated systems—that meet the needs of the small business owner—been available.

For those who don't work around other entrepreneurs, or are just getting started, they may not even know these systems exist. In fact, nearly a quarter of the conversations our sales representatives have with prospects lead to an exclamation like, "You can do that?" Yes, we can. Automation can. But unless you've been around it or heard someone discuss it, you may never have considered it for yourself.

Granted, there will be some things you'll never be able to automate; and you never should. But have a look at all the areas of your business that can easily benefit from the power of an automated system.

FOLLOW-UP

We don't want to be repetitive, so hopefully the last chapter gave you sufficient insight to the crucial nature of follow-up marketing. At this point, we're going to assume you agree with us—following up consistently with your prospects and customers is the fastest way to grow your business.

But when you don't even have the time to eat a meal or get a good night's sleep, how are you ever going to follow up with your contacts? Through automation. Automatic follow-up software gives you the power to manage emails, voice broadcasts, faxes and direct mail to any and all of your contacts. It launches predetermined follow-up sequences based on the actions of your contacts so that you're sending targeted communications rather than "shotgun communications." Furthermore, as part of a powerful contact management system, automatic follow-up software instantly executes and records every follow-up effort you make.

As long as you've invested the time in creating a valuable, educational, personal follow-up sequence, you're automatically doing the one thing you never thought you'd be capable of doing: You're leaving yourself time to close hot leads while your system is warming up a bunch of new leads for you.

Even if you were a follow-up master, you could not do as thorough and complete a job as your automated follow-up system can. If there are multiple steps in your marketing campaign, you're bound to make mistakes at some point. How do you know which contact receives what, and on which day? If you're only managing a handful of prospects, this can be done by a mere mortal. But once you have dozens, hundreds, even thousands of contacts to manage—you just can't do it anymore.

With automation, you get the benefits of follow-up without any of the pain or mistakes. Plus, you'll be building relationships that cannot be achieved any other way. For example, what if your system started this follow-up sequence once a new customer buys from you:

Day 1—Email: Thanks for your purchase. I appreciate you.
Day 8—Email: Let me thank you again for your purchase. Because you bought from me, I'd like to send you something special. Be watching your mailbox.

Day 15—Direct Mail: Thank you again, and here's a free gift for you. (This should cost you next to nothing.)

Day 30—Phone Call: Checking in to see if you're happy with your purchase.

Day 45—Post Card: Refer a friend and receive an extra discount on future purchases.

Think it would make a difference? You bet it will. That is the power of automation; and it works—magically. When Scott purchased a car two years ago, he received a thank-you call, a survey, a personalized note from the salesman, and two dozen cookies from a local bakery.

Scott's been working with automation a lot longer than two years. But he still appreciated the gestures made by this dealership. (And his kids appreciated the cookies. It was hard to explain to his four-year-old that he didn't need to buy another car to get his hands on more cookies.)

The great thing, is that automation is not limited to follow-up. It might be the best benefit to your business, but automation can cover nearly every aspect of your business.

Lead Capture

If you have a business, then you probably have a website. If you don't have a website, then you're working on getting one. Most people who visit your site are searching for information. If they don't find what they want on your website, they're forced to call you—taking up your precious time and theirs.

Well, if all they want is more information, why not begin the automated follow-up right from the start? Offer something of value on your website in exchange for a visitor's personal information. You could offer:

- A newsletter
- A free report or white paper

- A trial offer
- Membership in a special forum
- A demo of your product and/or service

The person came to your site looking for information. When you offer them that information in one of the forms above, they'll be more than willing to give you their name and email address. In fact, most people would prefer it since now they don't have to call you and bug you with more details about your products or services.

You don't have to do a thing, and you'll still be providing your visitor with invaluable information. You'll give them all the information they could ever want or need. Because now that you have their personal contact information in your database (which happens automatically when they fill out the form on your website), your system can automatically start sending them valuable, educational materials in one of your preplanned (and very effective) follow-up sequences.

We know we're simplifying how this process works in a big way, but once again, it's incredible! If you've never had an experience like this one, then take the time to go download a free report or white paper from someone's site.

BILLING AND COLLECTIONS

Years ago, we had a business owner call in who was extremely frustrated with her circumstances. She taught piano lessons from her home and really enjoyed what she was doing. As an accomplished musician, her reputation was impeccable and she had no difficulty in finding students. In fact, she often had a waiting list of those anxious to study under her.

So what was her frustration? She couldn't figure out how to get paid. Every time students attended a lesson, they were expected to bring their payment with them. But students frequently forgot. Sometimes personal checks bounced. If students missed a lesson, the teacher went unpaid (even with dozens of students waiting to be placed in her tutelage).

The answer to this challenge was—you guessed it—automation. She needed simply to automate her billing process. After getting her software set up (complete with a follow-up reminder sequence to her students), this new client was able to set up recurring charges for her services.

Each month, her entire list of students was billed through the credit card they had provided their teacher. Rather than bringing money with them to each lesson, students (and their parents) received an email letting them know that payment for the month had been charged. No longer did the business owner go unpaid or deal with bounced checks. When students missed a practice, they were charged the same as if they had attended their lesson.

On the rare occasion a credit card failed, automation went to work again. First, the piano teacher was notified of the failed charge attempt. Second, the system attempted to charge the card again a few days later. Third, a second failed charge sent another notification to the piano teacher. Fourth, an email was sent to the client asking them to contact the piano teacher immediately about their payment. The piano teacher never had to do a thing.

This very same automated billing and collection process can be set up in any business, and customized to meet the needs of the business owner. Maybe you want to set up a payment plan for a particular client. An automated system can do that. Perhaps you need to charge your clients on a quarterly or annual basis—no problem. Should you need to cancel a particular service in the case of failed payments, you can do that, too.

Rather than spend time every day working in your finances, simply automate the recurring and predictable billing processes. It's going to save you a whole lot of time, and once again, it keeps you from making mistakes.

WORKFLOW

Bottom line, with automation, you are making your business more scalable. Because things are set to run as needed, it really doesn't matter how many prospects and customers you add, the system can follow up with them all. You don't have to worry how many new accounts come in. The automated billing can handle thousands of clients.

Really, you can grow your business easily and effectively without growing your staff. However, sometimes the best choice for you is to add a few employees. If you offer a more expensive product or service, you might include a few sales representatives to handle all of the tricky issues once a prospect is eager and ready to buy.

But don't let the addition of a few employees make you think you don't need to automate every aspect of your business. Because you do. Managing workflow and managing your employees is easier than ever when you have an automated system in place.

With an automated system in place, you can:

- Automatically assign prospects to your sales reps
- Be notified as prospects move from one stage of the sales cycle to the next
- Enable sales reps to automatically respond to prospects' questions and concerns
- Instantly alert your employees when a sale is made (we love this one!)

This doesn't even begin to scratch the surface of the things you can do when you automate your workflow and the workflow of your employees. With just a little bit of assistance from an automated system, you can automate the customer fulfillment function of your business and maximize your time. How much time can you save just by keeping tabs on the tasks that need to be done, those that have been done, and those that should be done? Automation systems act as the production conveyor belt in your business, saving you time and sparing you from costly mistakes and manual labor.

We could go on and on about the capabilities of automating your business. However, until you experience it for yourself, it will be difficult to understand how easily it starts to pull you out of the chaos.

A STORY OF AUTOMATION

To help you see the potential for automation in your own business, we want to share one of our favorite stories with you. This story is the case study of our own customer. In March 2008 a husband and wife team won a contest we held for our customers and prospects. The prize was a year-long subscription for our automated marketing software.

When we first heard from this couple, they were a two-man shop, maxed out and wanting to grow their business. They had about 5,800 contacts on their list and they were receiving approximately 200 orders per month for their product. Although they were experiencing some growth, they knew their business had the potential to achieve more.

Well, we got them started with our automation software, and then sat back to watch the results. Within a single month of putting automation to work in their business, this couple began to see the benefits. First, their list of contacts grew, then their sales volume took off and with the automation tools in place, they were spending less time fulfilling orders.

Three months after implementing automated processes, their list size had grown to over 10,000 contacts, and they were receiving over 400 orders per month. The best part is that they weren't working longer hours, they hadn't hired any additional employees and they were less stressed than they had been three months prior.

Unfortunately, one year after putting automation to work, the wife had surgery that knocked her out of the business for a few weeks. Think about what would happen to your business if you were laid up with surgery. Would your business stagnate or thrive?

Here's what this customer said:

I had to have surgery in June, and I wasn't sure how long I would be out. Since our follow-up marketing sequences were already set to run on autopilot, there wasn't anything I had to do business-wise in order to prepare for my time off. Even though I wasn't in the office, new prospects received the information they were looking for, and the follow-up emails helped make the sales. *It ran like a machine.* We had record sales in June, even though I wasn't personally there much of the time. It is nice to know that if I ever need to take off an extended period of time, our family would still have a nice income coming in.

That is the power of automation. It's not just increasing sales, not just saving you time. Automation liberates and empowers entrepreneurs to live life on their terms. Oh, and by the way, at the end of the first year, with automation in place, this customer's business had grown to four times the original size.

- Their list size increased from 5,800 to 29,600
- Monthly sales volume went from 200 orders to 850 orders
- Monthly revenue shot from $13,000 to $48,000
- The only labor increase was some part-time help from their college-aged daughter

Honestly, we have no idea how anyone breaks free from the treadmill without automation. Automation can solve some of the most complex and time-consuming jobs a small business owner has to take on. And that gives the business owner the greatest advantage she can receive on her path to increased money, time and control.

So, you need to find yourself a system that keeps on working—even when *you* can't! Discover the power of automation, and you'll discover ways to simplify your business and significantly increase your revenue.

Section IV

FIND YOUR FREEDOM

10

AVOIDING THE BACKSLIDE

Changing an ingrained pattern, whether behavioral or emotional, is one of life's greatest challenges. Entrepreneurs like to think they eat obstacles for breakfast, and there's no shortage of gurus and pundits dishing out self-improvement advice. But real change is still very hard. As anyone knows who has ever made a resolution only to break it days later, it's easy to backslide.

—Alexander Stein, Ph.D.

S o this should be the part of the book where you breathe a sigh of relief. After all, there are only six strategies for getting out of the chaos: (1) Emotional Capital; (2) Disciplined Optimism; (3) Entrepreneurial Independence; (4) Centralize; (5) Follow-Up; and (6) Automate. They all make sense to you, and they all look fairly easy to implement. According to the standard rules of good books, it's time to feel that sense of empowerment, right?

As you've followed us through the strategies, you've learned what you need to find your freedom and:

- Make more money
- Find more time for yourself
- Take control of your own situation
- Achieve your purpose

You've learned everything you need to conquer the chaos and grow your business without going crazy. The knowledge you've acquired from this book has given you tools for making positive adjustments in both your business and your personal life.

As anxious as you are to get these strategies working in your business, it's not quite time to start celebrating. There are just a few final ideas we must share before you learn how to truly achieve the fulfilled life. (We'll save the celebrating for the next chapter.)

Once you've mastered these strategies, you have learned to conquer the chaos. But that does not mean you will never again be threatened by it. The elements that created chaos are still there. The speed at which technology moves does not slow down simply because you've learned to harness it. Customer demands are not going to stop just because you've taught yourself to be a disciplined optimist. It's an ongoing process that continues throughout the life of your business.

Let's take just a minute and talk about how to avoid sliding back into chaos. You see, once you've mastered the six strategies, there are three tendencies which are likely to shove you back onto the crazy treadmill if you're not careful. The three risks to steer clear of are:

1. The myth of long, hard work
2. Your unbridled ambition
3. The belief your business will fail without you

THE MYTH OF LONG, HARD WORK

Liberation itself is a fleeting feeling. The second you get free of chaos, you're going to take a deep breath of air and then feel a moment of panic. Without realizing it, you just broke free of the fear, self-doubt and agony of small business ownership. But instead of reveling in your accomplishment, you might feel like a fish out of water. You've been in chaos so long, you've become accustomed to it. In the most extreme cases, we've seen entrepreneurs who *need* chaos and who actually create it when it's not present in their businesses. Sound crazy? Stick with us.

We all know that hard work is an important contributor to success. With rare exception, those who achieve great things have worked very hard to get them. We are firm believers in the virtue of hard work. But have you ever considered that your work ethic might be contributing to the chaos?

Once you have the chance to step away from your business for a few hours, days and possibly even weeks, the work habits you have formed are no doubt going to haunt you. Even now, if you take a couple days off work, how do you feel? Agitated, grumpy even? It's because your mind is having a hard time computing your actions. It's saying, "Wait a minute! You don't just take time off work. You always work. Now what do I do about this?"

The problem is we have come to confuse long hours of work with productivity.

That's the myth. Somehow we fool ourselves into believing that if we just work longer hours, we will get more time, money and control (hah!). Worse yet, some of us feel like we don't deserve the time and money if we're not filling up a 60+ hour workweek with "work stuff." Why? So we can be busy just to be busy? It's not about hours spent; it's about productivity per hour spent.

But that's not the way our society is built. Nearly every job in Corporate America pays you for being present. Sure, there are a few progressive, entrepreneurial employers out there who pay you for your work product and don't care whether you're present, but those are the exception, not the rule.

The fact is, our society is wired to believe that hours spent at work translates to productivity and value. For that reason, you've got to fight not to fill your extra time with "stuff," not to slide back into the pit of chaos.

If you let yourself get tied down with the belief that long hours of work equals productivity, you will slip right back into chaos and your business will suffer. Once your systems are in place, give yourself the time you're saving. Don't make the assumption that you have to focus your efforts somewhere else.

While Clate was in high school, his mom worked part-time decorating model homes for home builders. When she needed furniture moved, Clate's mom offered him the opportunity to do the work. She paid him handsomely for his efforts, and on a "per-job" basis. Now although he can't say he was a huge fan of moving furniture, Clate recognized it could be very lucrative. Clate could rent a U-haul truck, pay a couple of buddies $10 per hour, and make $25 or $30 per hour. Clate had a good little enterprise going there for a couple years. But the key was that he wasn't paid hourly. He was paid to get the job done and he worked the business in such a way as to make it very profitable.

Now, while his friends slaved away at fast-food restaurants or retail stores, Clate worked a few hours a week and still made more money than they did. Did he give up his job because he didn't feel like he was working hard enough? Heck no! Did he give back the money because he felt he was being paid too well for his effort? Not a chance. Did he gloat a little bit to his friends? Yes.

Once you are outside the chaos, don't get tempted to jump back in. When you feel out of sorts because you find time on your hands, don't instantly search out something to do. It defeats the purpose of conquering the chaos.

Learn to use that time for yourself. If you want to work hard, good for you! Work hard helping your family, friends and community. But recognize that once the automation is working in your business, the long, hard work is no longer necessary. It's just a distraction—a sneaky trick to get you back into the long, tedious hours.

HARNESSING YOUR UNBRIDLED PASSION

The next challenge we want to caution you against is your own ambition. You see, a remarkable event occurs when the chaos is finally conquered. The entrepreneur reemerges. Once your business is running on auto-pilot and making you a whole lot of money, the entrepreneur is free to reign again.

Where did he or she go in the first place? Well, the needs of a small business are so demanding that the business owner has to be precisely that—a business owner. They haven't got the time to be creative or take risks. In dealing with continuous problems, they get bogged down by the business. Suddenly the creativity, excitement and passion of entrepreneurship are buried.

But, when the six strategies are put in place and the business becomes more effective, the entrepreneur has time to start dreaming about new possibilities. With some spare time on her hands she can think up new products or services, drum up some unique marketing ideas, and spend more time networking with other entrepreneurs.

With time to work on the business instead of *in* it, the possibilities for the entrepreneur are endless. Therein lies the problem.

Now that you find yourself with a lot more time, what's to stop you from taking on new projects? Too many new projects. When time and money are available, the floodgates open. You will be anxious to get your hand into a thousand new possibilities. Rather than focusing on your family, friends and personal life, the business will consume you . . . but in an all-new way.

You will no longer be fighting to:

- Pay the bills
- Make the sale
- Follow up with prospects

Instead, you will be fighting a million new ideas that all want your attention right now. Caught up in the excitement of liberation, far too many business owners give up the practical, realistic side of themselves and let the entrepreneur have free rein.

But if you're now focusing all your time on new projects, projects that need time, money and dedication, you're no longer liberated. You become a slave to those new ideas. And if you're not careful, your true purpose is lost.

Somehow, you've got to find the right balance between working on your business (a benefit of liberation), and going overboard with creativity. Remember, your family still wants you at home. Your friends are still hoping you'll have time to go out. Don't spend all of your newfound money, time and energy on re-investments in the business.

Don't get hung up believing that a passed up opportunity is something you're likely to regret down the road. Sure, you will have some of those, but in how many more situations will you be glad you bridled your ambition?

One of our mentors, Dan Sullivan, runs a coaching program for entrepreneurs called Strategic Coach. In his program, Dan teaches entrepreneurs to take "Free Days" away from the business. As an entrepreneur achieves more success, the number of free days she takes will increase. Keep that in mind and check your ambition by continually increasing the number of Free Days you take.

THE BELIEF YOUR BUSINESS WILL FAIL WITHOUT YOU

When you *first* started your business, you were the glue that held it all together. Without you there wasn't a business. The business only began because you saw a need to be fulfilled and you went for it. For the first few months or years, everything that got done was done because you did it.

You didn't start out with employees. You probably couldn't afford to hire a webmaster or copywriter. So you did it all. You may have had the help of a spouse or family members to assist—but for the most part it was you and your efforts.

If you stopped working, the business stopped working. If you weren't bringing in new leads, the business was not receiving any. If you didn't make sales, the business didn't make any money.

As a small business owner in chaos, that's the harsh reality. Without you, there is nothing. In fact, your business is probably branded with your name or other identifying characteristics. In other words, you are your business. Now it's time to get rid of the belief that everything depends on you.

The longer you've been in business, the more ingrained this belief is. You know, you can't just turn off the switch one day and say, "Hey, I've conquered the chaos in my business. It won't fall apart if I'm not there."

Think about the first time you ever took time away from your business. It could have been a single day. Maybe you decided to stop early on a Friday afternoon and go to a baseball game with your kids. Before leaving, you undoubtedly checked your voice mail, sorted through your email, checked your to-do list and cleaned up your desk.

Sounds like a good way to end the day. But before you actually walked out and locked the door, did you wait? Did you stand in the middle of the office waiting for it to fall apart? Were you listening for the phone to ring even as you walked out to your car? Did you immediately set up a redirect from your office phone to your cell phone?

None of these actions is surprising. Taking a step away can be a real struggle the first time. Even the second or third time. After that? You start to realize everything is fine when you're gone. Sure, sometimes fires pop up, but they would have popped up even if you had been there. And in almost every situation, you can take care of the fire when you're back in the saddle.

Relax. Let go. The business will be fine. In fact, we have found that it frequently thrives in our absence. Employees are glad to have a little more autonomy and decision-making power. The automation still runs whether we're there or not. In many cases, we and our customers have seen record productivity occur in our absence. It's not coincidence. The reality is that the business doesn't need you 24/7 like it once did.

That's a great thing! Enjoy it and don't re-position yourself in the middle of the business. When it comes right down to it, what is the point in conquering chaos if you won't let the business go once in a while?

Here's something you need to think about: you didn't start your business intending to be chained to it. Remember? You wanted freedom. Flexibility. The power to do what you want to do when you want to do it. Well, now you've got it. Don't squander it by succumbing to one of the three backslide threats.

Once you put the strategies into place, you've conquered the chaos. You have found the freedom you always dreamed of. You've achieved the Time, Money, Control and Purpose you wanted when you decided to go into business. What you don't want to do is take a step backward once you've come so far.

Chaos is always waiting for the opportunity to slip back into place. But as long as you know that, as long as you're watching for the warning signs of backslide, you can do something about it. When you need to, simply ask yourself what really matters in your life. Get back to the Hierarchy of Freedom and focus on the top level: Purpose. That's what you want. But every once in a while, even the best entrepreneur needs a reminder.

11

THE LIBERATED ENTREPRENEUR

In the bureaucratic world, people get paid for putting in time and effort. But entrepreneurs, who get paid only for how much value they create, regardless of what it took to get there, know that it's not how much time and effort you put in that counts—what matters is the result.
—Nomura, Catherine, and Sullivan, 2007

This is it—the chapter you read the entire book to reach. This is the chapter where you can start imagining life as a liberated entrepreneur.

As a liberated entrepreneur, all the pain and agony you have suffered, potentially for years, is gone. The mental, physical and social affects of running a company make a 180 degree turn. Instead of being bogged down by the business, you can allow yourself to enjoy it and even be energized by it. Because with the strategies in place, it is now a well-oiled machine where good things happen:

- You easily meet the needs of your customers and prospects
- You generate incredible amounts of income
- You find time to enjoy your family and friends (time you wouldn't even have if you were still working a 9-to-5 job)
- You are free to create

In an environment like this one, why wouldn't you want to go to work?

CLIMBING THE HIERARCHY OF FREEDOM

Now, just because you get things running a little better doesn't mean that you can sit back and coast. You still have to work.

But now the work is meaningful and productive rather than being the stuff that "gets you by."

As a liberated entrepreneur, you'll find you have:

- More money
- More time
- More control
- More purpose

Basically, you'll have what Jake's dad has—and so much more.

MORE MONEY

Wasn't the primary reason you went into business to make more money? Didn't you believe that with your knowledge and some hard work you could bring in more money than your old corporate job paid?

With the six strategies in place, a rapid increase in revenue is the first benefit you're going to experience. Through the processes and systems you put in place, you'll be maximizing every lead, every opportunity that comes your way. The strategies provide you with the tools you need to warm prospects, educate and provide value to your contacts and make the sales process a whole lot easier, and faster. If you can get a basic system in place—so you can stay focused on high-level ideas—you will see the sales come rolling in and the money piling up in your bank account.

Remember how Scott was told that the first million is the hardest to make? Well, it is. After nearly a decade of running our own small business, we can attest to that. But once you're making sales systematically, and you put the processes in place to more easily and effectively manage those sales, you start generating a whole lot more revenue. With the additional revenue, you can purchase more resources. With those resources, you can improve your systems and processes. And so the cycle continues with your bank account growing throughout the process.

When you can systemize your business and stay focused on the things you do best, your business will see an exponentially greater increase in sales, and you'll see an exponentially greater increase in your income.

MORE TIME

No matter what industry you are in, there is one truth that remains the same, systemization leads to time effectiveness. The more you can put processes into place, the better use you'll make of your time, your employees' time, your associates' time and your customers' and prospects' time.

That's why the System strategies are such an integral part of overcoming chaos. With the right tools in place, you can manage exponentially more contacts, bills and other work in your business. When you can get more done in less time, you can start making choices for yourself and your business. *You* can start deciding how much effort you want to put into a project or task.

Instead of running around at the bidding of your greatest demands, you have time to make plans. You can chart out years in advance where you want your business to be and what you are hoping to achieve. But more than that, you have the time to focus on what matters most.

One of Scott's neighbors works a typical 9-to-5 job. Unfortunately, the demands of his role frequently keep him working long hours. When Scott asked him what he was working so hard to achieve, he said, "Well, if I get caught up, then I'll have time to take a long vacation with my family."

Scott nodded his head and asked, "In the meantime, you're willing to give up the precious hours you could be spending with them each day? And somehow a week-long vacation is going to give it all back to you?"

The neighbor blurted out an incoherent response, but Scott was already on to his next question. "What are the odds that you will ever get fully caught up?"

The look in this man's eyes nearly broke Scott's heart. He knew better than anybody that work never ends. No matter how many projects you complete this week, there will be more projects to tackle next week. No matter how far ahead you think you're getting, there is always an infinite amount of "stuff" to be done.

As you implement these strategies, you will discover that your "spare" time comes from helping things run more smoothly. It comes from investing those initial hours to set up processes and systems that manage the bulk of your work for you . . . automatically.

The benefit of time is just waiting to be realized. The dream of doing what you want *when* you want is sitting on the horizon.

When you achieve an extra hour, day, week or month—because your business is running more effectively and your employees are learning to manage without you, you are truly liberated. You are no longer bogged down by the impossible demands of a chaotic business. The world is yours to conquer once again, like a true entrepreneur.

More Control

Perhaps the greatest benefit of using these strategies and overcoming chaos is the resulting control over your physical, mental and emotional needs. As you master the Mindset strategies in the book, the confusion and mess that are cluttering your mind and your life will be a thing of the past. The drained, wiped-out heap you form on your couch at night will be replaced with an energetic person, capable of taking charge of your own future.

It's not an easy thing to master the chaos in your head, but when you reach that state, you begin living deliberately.

You regain control of your business, because you're no longer reacting to it. Add to this the systems you put in place to run the business, and suddenly every move you make can be pre-determined.

With things running like clockwork, you can decide whether to:

- Add a new product
- Hire new employees
- Test a new process
- Spend more money on marketing
- Expand into a new market

Those are things you can decide, because the six strategies have given you control.

You've already freed yourself from the confines of the corporate world. Now it's time to break the chains of small business ownership. Only one force should be controlling your thoughts, actions and feelings—and that is you.

It doesn't make any sense to exchange one type of confinement for another. You wanted to live life on your terms. Well, when you choose to implement these ideas, you'll find that power in your hands.

MORE PURPOSE

We want to ask you something we asked at the beginning of the book. When you set out to grow a business, what were you hoping to achieve? The ideal lifestyle? A chance to "stick it to the man?" The freedom to be your own boss?

With the six strategies at your disposal, you can finally see your dreams develop. You will be the entrepreneur you hoped to become. You will be the success story that stands out among so many business failures. If you truly believe in and incorporate the strategies you've been given, your possibilities are endless. You can develop the type of company you always wanted—and live the lifestyle you earn.

Plus, as you reach that level of success, you'll start to realize your dreams are not limited to your business. You won't merely want to own a successful company. What you'll find is a greater purpose to what you're doing. Sure, time, money and control will go a long way in helping you find your freedom. But when you see your business running practically on it's own, you'll understand that your success has also given you the chance to give back to the world.

Perhaps you'll want to organize a charity, become a national speaker for your industry, or mentor other entrepreneurs. We cannot predict for you what your purpose will be. But you'll find it, and as a liberated entrepreneur, you'll be in a prime position to make the most of it. We have found in ourselves and in others that this higher sense of purpose brings entrepreneurs a level of satisfaction that can't be achieved through Money, Time or Control (the lower levels on the Freedom Hierarchy).

GIVING UP THE CHAOS

Once you have the strategies in place, the overwhelmed, neurotic behavior disappears. As situations in your business work themselves out, you're going to see things in a better, clearer light. Furthermore, as you tackle the Mindset strategies, you are prepared to handle any situation that comes up with a focused view.

With your business running on autopilot, you possess the power to think through situations. You can approach even unpleasant situations with a positive outlook. You find the energy to work through mistakes, overwhelming projects and other business situations.

Then, once you are able to *think* clearly, you also find the ability to:

- Eat on a regular basis
- Sleep more than 3 or 4 hours a night

- Walk away from the phone without panicking
- Empower your employees with the ability to do more
- Take a vacation (or several vacations)
- Enjoy the time you spend with your family
- Make good conversation during a social gathering
- Accept responsibilities outside of the office

But the best part is—you learn to become you again. You'll know the moment this happens. Old friends will make comments like, "It's nice to see you're doing so well." Or, "Ah, the old you is back again." Or, "I've sure missed the real you."

This experience through chaos will be extraordinary. You will come out of it a better, stronger person. You will have gained mental control that you might not have had before. You will learn how to use systems and processes to improve not only your business, but also your life. Furthermore, you will start to see the struggles and challenges of others in a whole new light.

You will be a more complete version of yourself. You'll have gone through the refiner's fire and come out on top. You will see the reemergence of your own life, only it's going to be a whole lot better. And now you will be more prepared than ever to live your dream.

So if the strategies work, why don't more entrepreneurs make the effort to overcome chaos? Because chaos is tricky. It has a way of making you think life isn't so bad—or, this is what small business ownership is all about—or, you understand this chaos so you're comfortable dealing with it.

Plus, these are not quick-fix solutions. They take time, dedication and a little bit of money to put in place. In order to break free from the chaos, you've got to break out of the daily routine and focus your efforts on a system that works for you.

Many entrepreneurs aren't ready to take those steps—in which case, the only thing we can do is wish those entrepreneurs luck. No one should have to cope with chaos. No one should be subjected to endless problems, mistakes and fear. As you can attest, it's not a pleasant existence. The face plant on the treadmill is not a pretty picture. We trust you won't allow that to happen to you.

Those who do find the answers, those who learn to incorporate

- Emotional Capital
- Disciplined Optimism
- Entrepreneurial Independence
- Centralization
- Follow-up
- Automation

in their businesses are the entrepreneurs who achieve true liberation. They are those who know that growth is the way to conquer chaos. They are those who know balance is achievable. They are those who are free to control their business instead of letting their business control them.

As you put these strategies to practice in your business and your life, you will accomplish your business ambitions and you will earn the liberation—the lifestyle—you've always wanted. Now go enjoy your freedom! And tell us about your success!

Appendix

SMALL BUSINESS RESOURCES

SMALL BUSINESS GROWTH ADVICE

This book provides you with the six strategies to conquer the chaos, but what do you do once you've implemented the strategies? You start working *on* your business rather than *in* your business. And sometimes when you start working on your business, you have a bunch of questions.

As an additional resource to this book, we invite you to join our small business growth newsletter. In this weekly newsletter, we teach the nine building blocks of small business growth. These techniques include:

- Supercharge Your Website
- Fill the Funnel
- Sell Stuff Online
- Growth Through Partners
- And More!

The information we share in the small business growth newsletter will help you discover and apply important techniques that will propel your business growth. Sign up for free at: http://www.conquerthechaosbook.com.

AUTOMATED FOLLOW-UP SOFTWARE

In Section III, you were encouraged to find systems for running your business. Although there are many "point" solutions available, including contact managers, email marketing programs, e-commerce and shopping carts, few of them combine all these modules into one centralized system. As you search for a solution, look for something that is:

- Designed specifically for small businesses
- Includes *all* the modules you need
- Provides you with excellent support resources
- Includes true automation

What you choose is entire up to you, and there are many systems available. If you would like to see Infusionsoft's Automated Follow-up System, and even sign up for a free trial to see how it works, please visit our website at: http://www .infusionsoft.com.

REFERENCES

Carnegie, Dale. 2009. *How to Win Friends and Influence People*. New York: Simon & Schuster.

Collins, Jim. 2001. *Good to Great*. London: Collins.

"Frequently Asked Questions." SBA—Choose Public SBA System. http://web.sba.gov/faqs/faqIndexAll.cfm?areaid=24 (accessed December 15, 2009).

Gerber, Michael. 1995. *The E-Myth Revisited: Why Most Small Businesses Don't Work and What to Do about It*. New York: Harperbusiness.

Hill, Napoleon. 2009. *Think and Grow Rich*. London: Createspace.

Kennedy, Dan S. 2006. *The Ultimate Marketing Plan*. Avon: Adams Media.

Nomura, Catherine, and Dan Sullivan. 2007. *The Laws of Lifetime Growth: Always Make Your Future Bigger than Your Past (Bk Life)*. San Francisco: Berrett-Koehler.

Peale, Norman Vincent. 1955. *The Power of Positive Thinking*. 14th ed. New York: Prentice-Hall.

"Quotations of Theodore Roosevelt by The Theodore Roosevelt Association." About Theodore Roosevelt: President and more, from The Theodore Roosevelt Association. http://www.theodoreroosevelt.org/life/quotes.htm (accessed December 17, 2009).

"Strategic Coach®: Work less. Make more money. Do what you love. Freedom for entrepreneurs." Strategic Coach®: Work less. Make more money. Do what you love. Freedom for entrepreneurs. http://www.strategiccoach.com (accessed December 17, 2009).

About the Authors

CLATE MASK

Clate Mask is the CEO and co-founder of Infusionsoft, the leading provider of marketing automation software for true small businesses. His passion is helping small businesses grow, and over the years, he has spoken to tens of thousands of small business owners.

Clate received his Bachelor's of Science in Economics from Arizona State University in 1996. He also completed his Master's of Business Administration and Juris Doctor from Brigham Young University in 2000.

In addition to his work at Infusionsoft, Clate enjoys serving his community. He served for many years as a Scoutmaster and is on the advisory board for the Never Again Foundation.

Clate is the author of two popular eBooks, *The Edge of Success: 9 Building Blocks to Double Your Sales* and *The New Entrepreneur's Guide to Follow-up*.

When Clate isn't working to build Infusionsoft, he loves to spend time with his gorgeous wife and six great kids. In 2007, he was awarded the "Father of the Year Award." The balancing act can be difficult at times, but his family supports him 100 percent and serves as a constant reminder about what really matters in life. As much as Clate loves to write and execute a good business plan, his real joy comes from the time he spends with them.

SCOTT MARTINEAU

Scott Martineau is the co-founder and VP of Product Management at Infusionsoft. He feels strongly that entrepreneurs need to stop looking around and doing what everyone else is doing. Instead, he suggests they find their own mission in life and go build a great company around that dream.

Scott received his Bachelor's of Science in Computer Information Systems from Arizona State University in 2000. He was accepted to law school but chose to become an entrepreneur instead.

Outside of work, community spirit is very important to Scott. Between helping his wife with her homeschooling activities, his efforts in the scouting program, and helping others research their family history, Scott has his hands full. Plus, Scott's family recently moved into a more rural area of the city. He describes himself as a "city boy who's gone country," and he's having a great time caring for horses, chickens, cats, and dogs.

In his spare time, Scott loves to watch and play basketball, play with his six children (throwing stuff, wrestling, dancing, computer games, reading stories, etc.), and go on dates with his beautiful wife.

INDEX